BLUNT FORCE

BLUNT FORCE

A Reporter's Heartbeat

Gary L. Wilson

VANTAGE PRESS
New York

Copyright © 2009 by Gary L. Wilson

Published by Vantage Press, Inc.
419 Park Ave. South, New York, NY 10016

Manufactured in the United States of America
ISBN: 978-0-533-16034-1

Library of Congress Catalog Card No: 2008903071

0 9 8 7 6 5 4 3 2 1

Dedicated To

Joyce Louise Muro Wilson

. . . who loved, supported, guided and
taught me life's knowledge through
19,689 days of a graceful marriage.

Contents

Preface
Gutless, Guilty and Grimy
(A Thirty-Year Reporter's Notebook)

If you're not interested in how you're being screwed by your so-called leaders and their lackeys, this is not a book for you.

This one tells it with the Emperor's lack of brains, dirty dealings, laziness, self-interest and naked humor exposed. Most of the people are so inept that if they had no power over other folks' lives we'd all be laughing until our ribs ached.

I saw it all. Graduating from Bowling Green State University January 29, 1954, I went to work noon the 30th at WICA AM, FM and TV in Ashtabula, Ohio. About two years later I discovered the station manager, who had been there since 1939, was making only five dollars a week more than I was! I asked the owner how long it would be before I made $100 a week. His answer was, "never."

Two weeks later, I was working for WWCA AM in Gary, Indiana. Two years later WGRY AM, Gary before it became WLTH, two years later WJOB AM, Hammond, Indiana, four years later *The Times* of Hammond, a year later Manager of Press Relations for Northern Indiana Public Service Company, seven years later *The Times* again, two years later on a picket line and finally from 1978 to 1982, back at WJOB.

As for the short-time stints at three consecutive radio stations, I will only say I worked for three station owners who were seriously close to being outside the normal limits of sanity. One forced his own son to drive announcers to and from the county fair when he was suffering so much with hay fever he could hardly see; another would cry while writing checks for payday; yet another made a serious attempt to pay a waitress to go to bed with him while he was sitting at the table with two newsmen and his *wife*.

Word is reporters become cynical very quickly.

With me it took a few weeks.

Fictional police reports, fires for hire, open gambling and so on. Big stories while in Ashtabula would include the Andover Disaster, a theater fire and a big new dock dedicated in Ashtabula Harbor by the R.W. Sidley Co.

At the last, a United States Senator asked me, "Why are we here?" I said "To dedicate this dock." Five minutes later the Senator got up and spoke for thirty-five minutes concerning what a great development this was for Northeastern Ohio.

My introduction to the shallow frailty of political depth—"Give 'em the development speech."

Two years later as still a young newsman arriving in Gary, Indiana, to work at the dominant radio station in the city, it did not take me long to determine it was a corrupt town under anyone's definition of the word.

The first clue presented itself as I sat down near the middle of the counter in a diner on the city's main street about six stools to the right of a uniformed Gary policeman. To his left the counter ended giving access to an open door behind the counter leading to a back room. From where I sat, I could easily hear the sounds of a slot machine.

Cop, a lot nearer the door than me, coolly sipped his coffee.

Never moved.

I thought he was either deaf or the fix was in.

Since he talked in normal volume to the counterman, I opted for the fix.

Fixes equate to corruption.

Within the first week I knew the location of The Big House and the "Black Gold" Lucky Strike Policy Wheel (Illegal gambling) and the M & J Motel, Venus Café, Four Aces, Chesterfield Club (the largest of scores of houses of ill repute). I also had discovered how much it would cost to cut a curb for a driveway. The fee was $1,100—$100 for each Democrat councilman and $300 for the mayor.

So you will read the stories of the legends from inside. Mayors Pete Mandich, George Chacharis (Cha-Cha), Walter Jeorse, Lake County Prosecuting Attorney Metro Holovachka, Civil Defense Director Zenon R. "Bud" Bardowski, head of the 1950s version of Homeland Security and just as useless.

Governmentally Cha-Cha, Jeorse and Holovachka were the troika that ran the county. They did it by working closely with the real powers—the U.S. Steel Corporation and other large taxpayers and the outfit.

For instance, every morning representatives of U.S. Steel Corp. showed up at the Gary police station. If the cops had arrested someone the corporation needed to work that day he walked, be it open hearth, coke ovens or bridge division. Then there was Gaetano "Tommy" Morgano who, later, was proved in court to be the enforcer for the Outfit. "One Arm" Jimmy whose word was life or death on the strip in Calumet City, Illinois. And others, bright and dim, who populated our world.

There's also the never-told story of JFK and a new suit; Bobby Kennedy and his stupid (and expensive) ego; The Andover, Ohio explosion that killed 22 people; and more.

Not everything these people did was bad. There was some good mixed in.

And there were some great people in "Da Region." Dr. Hedwig Kuhn and her clinic and the Hammond Safety Council comes to mind along with Officers Les Downing and Clint Savage (Bugalske and Blamire were the odd couple in Hammond's Police Department), Norman "Bob" Borne, Richard Pontney. . . .

We'll tell their stories too.

After covering more than 100,000 such yarns I find it difficult to choose the eighteen or so most informative and entertaining, but I'll try.

Of course you have the right to know why this book has been written—the motivation of the author.

The answer is to counter layer upon layer of propaganda fed the public over the years.

Officer Friendly is really not friendly at all.

No teacher really likes a bright student.

The U.S. stopped being a "republic" at the end of the Civil War.

Equal justice for all is not only a joke—it's impossible.

So take my hand and we'll return to a time when there were actual reporters, not people who made a "phone" call. Where editors demanded facts, not opinions, and where men like Jim Brahos, Clint Wilkinson, Jep Cadue and Rich Fischer ran working newsrooms.

You'll read about what abortions were like when they were illegal; a great church where fire destroyed both ends of the building but left a newly remodeled center section untouched; Opal Collins; George Robert Brown; and the murky meanderings of several police departments.

The slippery sands of ever-changing laws to ensnare the unwary—sort of like trying to play a game of Monopoly with the rules changing every time you moved around the board. Done purposely? You better believe it. Every inane law generates money for governments, attorneys, jailers, courthouse clerks, police and the other parasites of our society. They will eventually "kill the goose that lays their golden eggs." Check your history books.

Let's start with John F. Kennedy, his trip to thank the thieves who stole an election for him and a reporter's incredible piece of luck.

Fun and games in the Windy City.

BLUNT FORCE

An Inside Peek
at the Ones Who Govern . . .

A New Suit

The boss said, "Tomorrow you're going to meet the President."

I said, "Like hell I am. I don't even have a suit."

This was back in the radio days of the early sixties where they gave you a meaningless title which took you out of the wage and hour law, and then worked you seventy or eighty hours a week for pennies.

It seems John F. Kennedy was going to make his only speech outside Washington, D.C. in Chicago's McCormack Place to thank Mayor Richard Daley and his minions for snatching victory from defeat in the 1960 election. Somehow I had been tabbed to provide the play by play for nine radio stations and three TV stations.

Pool coverage dictated by tier space.

The boss, Julian Colby, owned WJOB which was and is the only AM radio station in Hammond, Indiana. He solved the suit problem by taking me to the nearby Woodmar Shopping Center and bribing a clothing store manager into fitting me up with a new suit in one day.

Net result, I'm on the South Shore rattler for the Loop on a Friday morning, April 28, 1961, headed for Randolf Street and a walk over to Daley's office for the assignment's credentials.

"May I help you, sir?" the pleasant-looking lady in back of the desk inquired.

"Yes, I'm here to pick up reporter's credentials for the President's address at McCormack Place." I gave her my Chicago Press Card and visor parking permit. The visor card, about the size of a license plate, was attached to the underside of the sun visor on the driver's side of a reporter's vehicle and could be turned down showing a beat cop the car belonged to a working reporter. They were closely guarded and not used frivolously by any reporter I ever knew.

"Have a seat over there," she directed. "It'll be a moment."

Two *hours* later I told her I was going to lunch and would be back.

When I returned a different lady was behind the desk: "May I . . ."

"I'm the reporter from Indiana waiting for Presidential appearance passes for McCormack Place tonight," I said.

"Oh, yes. Here you are."

She handed me an envelope. In it was the Press and parking pass I had given the first lady and a note: "I'm sorry. Mr. Klien has been *very* busy. Perhaps the President's aides can give you the passes you need."

Of course, I had no clue how to come up with a "President's aide" so, with no idea of what to do, I decided to visit a friend, Vern Vessily, who worked at ABC Vending-Confection Cabinet a couple blocks north on Ontario Street. He was a major Chicago contact as well as a friend. The companies supplied food and beverages for most of the nation's ballparks and made founder Manny Smerling a wealthy man. Mr. Colby married Mr. Smerling's only daughter. That's how Mr. Colby got the money to buy WJOB and in a roundabout way how I got to meet Mr. Vessily.

I never asked Vern what his job was with the company, but I did find out he could get me tickets for anything you couldn't buy tickets for in Chicago at face value plus ten percent. *Maybe*, I thought, *he might be more help to me than the office of his honor the Mayor.*

I walked into his second floor office and was immediately introduced to the head of the President's *secret service detail!*

"Hey, good to see you, kid," Vessily said. "How come you're in town? Meet Don Rhodes. Did you know the President's gonna be in town tonight? Don heads up his security."

"Well, yes," I answered Vessily while shaking hands with the man seated at Vern's desk and doing my best to look like this was just an everyday occurrence. "I'm supposed to handle the pool broadcast of the President's speech tonight, but I can't seem to get passes for McCormack Place."

"Passes? Credentials? For tonight?" Chief Rhodes slid open one of the desk drawers. "Here's a parking pass for the south lot, tier pass, floor pass, directions for reporters at the airport . . . You going to the airport? . . . President's itinerary, motorcade route to McCormack. That do it? What else do you need?"

I stood there holding the stack of printed material Rhodes had casually tossed into my hands unable to believe my luck! More than two wasted hours at city hall and nothing. My problem solved in less than two minutes in Vessily's office.

"No. No airport or motorcade for me, sir. Now that I can get in I've got to head over to McCormack and set up for tonight. I don't know what they have there to hook up to and I need to be 'on the air' when the man walks in."

I thanked them both more than once, noted the three black Lincoln limousines at the loading dock apron with new insight as I left the building and hailed a cab for the ride to the hall. I had taken no special notice of the Presidential limos going into the building—black limos were not an unusual sight around Smerling's headquarters. (Although they were usually Cadillacs.)

As for the evening, there were more than a thousand guests at $100 a plate; forty-five-minute reception with people swirling around JFK; the meal; introduction of every Demo in Cook County of any note; and a short speech by the leader of the free world. I don't remember a single thing he said that night, nor do I recollect seeing Mrs. Kennedy. She may have been present, but out of sight.

What I do remember is how Kennedy stood out in the middle of that crowd of people. Looking down from the tier you could easily follow the reddish gold hair in a sea of dark brown, black and gray.

Boy, came the unwanted errant thought, *what a target . . .*

I caught the 1:15 A.M. train back to East Chicago—closest stop to the radio station amid the crazy quilt town borders—the last eastbound train for the night. It's the one that carries the men and women back home from the office buildings they clean for the daytime folks. The people are tired, dressed in work clothes and completely natural. It was a warmer, more caring crowd than the expensively dressed group at the gathering I had recently left. They obviously knew and felt concern for each other and were happy to be going home.

"See you tomorrow, Mother," the young lady said to an older woman as she left the train at Hegewisch. "Have a good night, love," the older lady replied. There were hugs and cheerful expressions of care at Hammond ten minutes later and at East Chicago where I also departed the train, but I'm sure the same scene was repeated later at Bridge Street, Gary and Michigan City, the end of the line for this train each night.

There was no way not to notice the wide contrast between the two groups of people I was with that night. The difference between wealth and modest means was, of course, obvious. But beyond that was in all probability the fact the one group was together once or at most a relatively few times in a lifetime and could show almost any "face" they wanted to project.

The other was together every morning. No pretense here. It's one great separate family that exists only between 1:15 and 2:00 A.M. when the work is done.

As I drove toward the radio station to write up and record a report for the overnight newscasts, I decided I liked both groups: the one that included Vessily, Manny Smerling, Chief Rhodes and the overdressed, self-important crowd at McCormack, and the one with a woman who was called "Mother" by a tired but caring young lady who was obviously no relation.

The program the President signed for me that night along with the Tier Pass, reporter's instructions and so on are in a bank lock box—a signature with lots of provenance.

I learned a lot of lessons this day: private enterprise trumps bureaucracy at least in the Chicago Mayor's office, sheer luck is greater than pre-planning and your standing in society doesn't really matter since the real genuine people seemed to be on a southbound train in the early morning hours of Saturday.

I wore the "new" suit on three other occasions before it began to fall apart.

Ok, let's take a look at another type of luck that maybe saved the economic base of an Illinois City. I call it . . .

Almost the Luckiest Mayor

For a few years, I thought Mayor Joseph W. Nowak of Calumet City, Illinois, was the luckiest man since Enoch went up with God!

Mayor Edward Dowling of Hammond, Indiana, had watched the closing of the Erie, Monon, Indiana Harbor Belt Railroad yards in his city and the town had tanked. Without the $8,000,000 payroll spent in the hotels, drug stores, clothing stores, restaurants and so on in his city, they closed down.

The tax base also took a major hit. All Dowling had where there once was a busy rail hub was fifteen or twenty acres of sand, gravel and scrub grass. Years later a gated community of half a dozen upscale homes paying, in comparison, pennies in property taxes was developed.

The downtown area shrunk to a major hospital, a utility company headquarters, a couple of banks and the largest Baptist Church in the United States. More than fifty other businesses left town or closed completely.

Now, Nowak had run and won for mayor of the Outfit's most lucrative town this side of Covington, Kentucky, without the faintest idea of how he would keep his promise to shut down the infamous State Street strip row. I asked him how he was going to get the mob to "ok" closing the strip palaces along State Street and its intersecting State Line Avenue between Indiana and Illinois and stay alive.

He told me he had no idea.

So I inquired how he would replace the $12,000,000 to $15,000,000 tax base supplied by the flow of money from the alluring ladies and the sin strip that bought police cars, fire trucks, heated and cooled city hall and mostly paid the workers therein. I got the same answer.

I went away shaking my head.

State Street in Cal City was at least as well known in the region as Wrigley Field, Union Station and the Palmer House! It had introduced legions of young mid-American males to the contours of the feminine body in motion. While the ladies stripped themselves of various articles of clothing, their assembled audiences were stripped of cash, coin, and sometimes conscience.

A few weeks later in John's Restaurant, while eating a bowl of the best minestrone ever served, I stared in wonder at hearing the biggest part of Nowak's problem in the process of possibly solving itself.

"One Arm" Jimmy ran State Street and all its people from the Paradise Club on Plummer Street one block north and running parallel to State Street and the girly joints. Jimmy lost his arm at Commonwealth Edison's State Line Generating Station by inserting himself between two 440 volt terminals. His arm was scorched when the amperage involved threw him across the room breaking the connection. Unemployed, and with only one arm, jobs were hard to find with thousands of able men returning at the end of World War Two. He had no trouble saying yes to the boys when they offered him command of the strip.

But now, 18 years later, it seemed he was tired of it.

"It's been some time and the paint's fading," I heard him tell a fellow diner. "If I can get the votes, we'll close this faded lady down and go for bigger profits. I'd rather milk cows on the farm than these cows up here."

His plans, he confided, were to retire to some acreage he had purchased several years before in downstate Indiana. This was a time when newer, apparently more profitable and less gaudy joints were opening up in Cicero and other nearby villages.

Wow, I thought, as I left the restaurant, *if Jimmy gets his way State Street will close itself.*

Little did I know Nowak's second problem was being cleared up by planners from Sears, Roebuck and Company. They were finding out that the greatest concentration of discretionary money in the Chicagoland area was right in his hip pocket—Chicago's southern suburbs and the adjacent northwest Indiana mill and heavy industry towns. They also found a 100 acre site with good roads and infrastructure right in the middle of all that money—a part of Thornton Township on the southwest border of Calumet City south of the Green Lake preserve!

There was just one problem. It was unincorporated.

Attorney John B. Austin, Sears PR man, proposed a multi-million-dollar shopping center at Torrence Avenue and 159th Street in Calumet City if the town would just annex the land assuring city services.

Talk about a replacement tax base!

They had solved Nowak's second problem, but given him three more. Well, the first really wasn't really a problem. The mayor would have to sign the agreement with Sears. The mayor was leading the charge.

The second was annexation of the land then a part of Thornton Township and the third rezoning the land from single family dwellings to business. Illinois State Law at the time required any land annexed by a city had to come in zoned single family.

The later two took public approval along with other governmental nods. In both private and public sessions the same night the fourteen-member city council voted unanimously in favor of the annexation.

The first public hearing was set for April 23 of 1964 in

the council chambers of the old stone city hall on Pulaski Street. Sears promised a two-story 250,000 square foot retail center and predicted two theater buildings, several restaurants, a free standing Marshall Fields store and many more.

Nowak was looking at tax revenues in the tens of millions per annum.

It was practically a pre-riverboat casino!

As a matter of fact, so often occurring when great amounts of money are involved, such minor matters as public protests and grumbling from Thornton Township officials were easily swept aside.

At the opening of the huge River Oaks Shopping Center, Major Joe took full credit for the revitalized Calumet City with a tripled city budget, large increases in employment in both the public and private sectors and, of course, a place in history for Joseph W. Nowak. "We won't miss the revenue of a closed State Street sin strip," he crowed, looking directly at me.

Perhaps he should have given a little verbal nod to the Outfit when it came to the shuttering of the strip clubs. Within a year Nowak was caught taking a bribe and wound up serving prison time.

There is no doubt in my mind who gets the credit for that.

A month later City Editor Clint Wilkinson threw a few bucks from petty cash at me and told me to ". . . go find out where the dolls are shedding outer garments in this new era."

I said, "Save the loot, Chief. You've got The Sultan's Table over in East Chicago, Kenny May's Seven Seas in Hammond across the street from the Federal Court House and a string of stages along Cicero Avenue in south Chicago. You can buy lap dances supine, sitting or standing, drugs, girls and good food and drink."

"How the hell you know this stuff?" Clint asked.

"You pay me to know that stuff along with gambling—bar butte, dice and cards at the Olympic Billiards, girls working out of the Jefferson Hotel across the street from our loading dock and the LaSalle on Hohman Avenue down the street. I'm your Hammond beat reporter."

"Gimme two books," he said.

In newspaper parlance a "book" is a page of triple spaced copy with two carbons.

May told me later attendance at his Seven Seas Club went up 15 percent after the piece hit the street.

I should have asked him for a cut.

Of course, most people didn't mourn the loss of the flesh palaces on State Street. Sometimes people got lost out there with no one really knowing what happened to them. Dottie was a good example of this back in my radio days at WJOB.

"Different government" officials involved here, but just as committed, decisive and secretive.

They may not have three million pages of secret documents as our federal government does, but there are details we may never know. . . .

Missing . . . Still Missing

The call came at 1:20 A.M. Saturday morning and the man on the phone was crying.

"She's not home," he said between sobs when I answered the newsroom phone.

"Neither am I," I said. The council budget committee had gone overtime. It was 1:30 A.M. and I had just completed the story for the overnight newscasts and my mind was on home, bed and a couple hours sleep before I was due back for the 6 A.M. news.

"She always comes straight home when the last show ends or calls me. Nothing. Something's wrong."

"Who's she? And what show? You're not making sense, man."

"She's my wife Dottie and she does an act in Cal City, but she's not a stripper. Never strips. It's a performance. . . ."

"Well, calm down, man. She probably got delayed. Tell you what . . . if she still hasn't turned up when I get back in the morning, I'll look into it. Have you reported her missing to the police?"

"Are you kidding? They won't do anything. We're talking Cal City police!"

"Ok, check with you in the morning, Uh . . . later this morning."

We left it at that and I went home for sleep, shower, shave, change and a quick bite before returning to work via the stop at the cophouse on the way. No report of a missing female.

After the Saturday cycle of morning news reports, I called the number and asked if Dottie had turned up.

His "No, she hasn't" sounded fatalistic. Like he had already accepted that there was no hope. Maybe he knew something I was not aware of.

"Well, buck up, man," I said. "I'll see what I can find out this evening."

Nothing really stirred much on State Street until sundown, but I went a little earlier and talked to a couple of drivers at the cab stand and realized I was going to need a picture of the woman if I expected to get anywhere.

I called the man, doubled back to his home on Rimback Street in Hammond and he gave me a publicity photo of a slim, dark blonde woman of, I thought, about thirty years old. It looked like he had gotten even less sleep than me. I had seen her act. He was right. She did not strip. When her left side was toward the audience, she was a man dressed in a tux. When her right side was to the spectators, she was a blonde woman dressed in a bright red gown. She began the show as though the "two" were dancing. During the course of the act the "man" raped the "woman." For Calumet City this was a class act.

It was late enough now that "One Arm" Jimmy would be in his Paradise Club on Plummer Street. I had to ask for his permission before questioning people about the girl. Jimmy ran the street, and you collected certain risks if you nosed around the State Street strip joints without his ok.

I got his approval to talk to people and a disclaimer of any knowledge on his part as to what might have happened to delay her return home.

She was performing at the Show Club on State, when she vanished; so I started there. Nope, no hassle, the barkeep said, nothing unusual, quiet night, appreciative crowd. The way he said it let me know Jimmy's word had preceded me. However, the man hired to maintain order in the club, bouncer in the vernacular, told me to "drift." I told him Jimmy said I could ask about her. He said, "Drift anyway."

So I left after telling him I'd be back to talk to some of the strippers if need be. He showed me a fake grin.

A waitress at John's restaurant out for a smoke said she knew Dottie and saw her walking briskly toward State Line Avenue at about 1:05 A.M. Waved to her, but did not exchange words.

Pay dirt back at the cab stand. A driver who had come on at 6 P.M. named "Toby" told me he saw her getting on the 1:10 A.M. southbound Greyhound bus.

He thought it "odd."

"Generally steps right on by," he said, "with a wave and a scent of perfume on the morning air. Makes you wish you had gone to college and could afford something like that."

I told him, college don't always cut it: went home, caught a nap, changed clothes, and was waiting Sunday morning when the driver eased to a stop.

"This bus keep the same schedule every morning, including Sunday?" I asked.

"Yep," he said, "same old run."

"You driving last night?"

"No, that would have been Frank. Take a seat, please, next stop Dalecarlia."

Then Kankakee and so forth until Champaign-Urbana then the home of the Fighting Illini. At each stop I left the bus, showed the picture and asked the station agent, if there was one, or the handyman loading luggage, or anybody else that might have been there the night before if they had seen our girl. All negative until C-U. There the station agent took the picture and told me: "Yeah, a looker. She got off . . ." And the phone rang in back of the counter. "Scuse me, gotta get that," he said. When he picked up the phone and had listened for a few seconds he looked over his shoulder at me. "You by any chance Gary Wilson?" he asked.

I nodded. He said, "This is for you. You can lift that flap over there . . ."

At first it seemed impossible. I hadn't told anyone where I was going. How could anybody call me here? Then I figured somebody must have seen me getting on the bus in Cal City and would know by the schedule that if I was still on it I would be in Champaign-Urbana.

When I got to the phone the voice said, "You know who this is?"

"I'm quite sure I do," I replied.

"You're wasting your time," he said.

"But I'm trying to trace . . ."

"You're wasting your time," he repeated and hung up.

I headed back for the Calumet area disappointed with myself that I had to be told twice.

The husband and children had moved out of their apartment by the time I made it back. Landlord and neighbors all said there was no coercion in the move. They had just left.

The voice on the phone was not to be challenged by a reporter for a teakettle radio station or for that matter hardly anyone. He was to insiders the head of the Chicago Outfit. In some areas it's called the mob, or wise guys, or the family—very seldom referred to in my experience as the Mafia.

The girl was not heard from again in the region. She *may* be happily performing in Vegas, or L.A. or Covington, Kentucky, rejoined by her children and tearless husband.

That's what I like to believe.

Perhaps you would like to follow me back to Indiana and meet a different kind of official.

The Invitation Got Lost in a Bar

The powerful Kennedy clan was interested in seeing Bethlehem Steel Company build a billion dollar mill at the southern tip of Lake Michigan in the Indiana Dunes between Gary and Michigan City.

Mayor George Chacharis of Gary, not wanting competition so close to his city's largest taxpayer—U.S. Steel Corporation—was bitterly opposed to the idea.

Initially the Kennedys didn't take much notice of the opposition by a relatively unknown small town leader in Indiana. That all changed, as they say, in the twinkling of an eye when Cha-Cha persuaded U.S. Senator Paul Douglas (D. Ill.) and the Save the Dunes Council ladies to join his team of city and county officials. After Douglas arranged a helicopter tour of the Dunes area for some sixty officials, conservationists and reporters, the Kennedy forces were jolted into action.

And things went terribly awry for the locals.

Bobby Kennedy, our nation's chief lawman with the solid backing of his all powerful brother the President, decided it was time to persuade the locals of the undeniable good the Kennedy interest would bestow on the region. The mighty man called Gary City Hall to arrange a meeting with Chacharis, but he didn't get Chacharis. He got an aide to the mayor and told him to relay the word that United States Attorney General Robert Kennedy would be at the Drake Hotel in Chicago the next day at 3 P.M. and expected Chacharis to be there to meet him.

The flaw in this arrangement was that the man who

took the message (whose name oddly enough was also Kennedy) was an alcoholic. He went on a three-day binge and forgot to inform his honor about the meeting.

Bobby Kennedy flew into O'Hare International Airport on a Friday afternoon, set up at the Drake to dazzle the hick mayor from the banks of the Little Calumet River . . . and as far as he knew was deliberately stood up.

People who should know told me Bobby waited a couple of hours, temperature rising minute by minute! Word from the hotel folk was that by the time Bobby left the building his wake sucked half the furniture out with him. At O'Hare Airport they said his plane took off for Washington, D.C. without cranking up the engines.

These are possibly little bitty exaggerations, but the point holds: the second most powerful man in U.S. government felt he had been publicly humiliated. Yessir, Vice President Lyndon Johnson admitted publicly he was in Bobby's shadow—he was number three.

Now the Kennedys are not the most intelligent people who have walked on earth. A simple call the next Monday morning could have smoothed the troubled brow of Kennedy the younger. Alas, that was not his style.

Saturday morning there were <u>126</u> *Federal Excise Agents in Lake County, Indiana.*

It seemed half of them were in my newsroom. Local source for places to start their "investigation." They were not shy in telling me they were there to get something on Mayor George Chacharis. I told them, politely I think, that they didn't need $50,000 a day in salaries paid by taxpayers to get something on the mayor. I told them a reasonably bright six-year-old could do it.

They left me alone for the most part after the first couple of days.

And in about two months, or so, they coerced, persuaded, blackmailed or plea bargained someone from Shamrock Engineering to testify his company kicked back forty percent of the bid price on a construction project to the city officials.

The Feds then indicted Chacharis and almost everybody he knew for ignoring one of the myriad laws passed to keep public officials honest while dealing with those they swear to protect.

I thought at the time about a trillion dollars unaccounted for in the Bureau of Indian Affairs while the full weight of our government was going after a mayor over a few thousand dollars.

". . . and equal justice for all."

They used the "slamming of the doors" technique at Cha-Cha's trial in Federal Court at Hammond. This consists of proving a person's net worth and then "slamming" all the ways he or she could have honestly gotten the money. It is a long, tedious process. Couldn't have made it in salary, investing, inheritance, won the lottery, found laying on the sidewalk, given to him by a friend or family member and on and on.

After months of this sort of thing at taxpayer's expense, they offered George a bargain. If he would plead "guilty" and spend a little time in jail, they'd let all the rest of his co-defendants walk.

George was the only one on trial who was not married.

He agreed. His friends and relatives went home.

The story fell from the headlines.

When the "troika" ran the county a person could walk the streets in relative safety, Gilroy Stadium was built, Indiana Avenue (now Martin Luther King Drive) was completed as a through street and families could swim in Lake Michigan where now stands rusting steel mills and other industrial development. The original interlopers, the Bailly and Michigan City generating stations of the Northern Indiana Public Service Company, have been joined not only by Bethlehem Steel but also National Steel, Midwest Steel and the Indiana Harbor.

As for Gary, Indiana, go see for yourself. From Indiana's second largest city to almost a ghost town all within the twentieth century. In one year more than 300 business permits were issued by officials of Merrillville, a town two miles south of Gary. Most of the new businesses, including the *Gary Post-Tribune,* dropped the "Gary" from their firm name. The separate town of East Gary became Lake Station.

The environmentalists got the Indiana Dunes State Park enlarged and a brand new Indiana Dunes National Park.

Maybe Bobby's troops could have saved some time and taxpayer dollars by talking with Ted Root. . . .

The Phantom Trailer Park

Ted Root owned a trailer park on Gary's near east side with easy access to both the downtown area of the Steel City and the sandy beaches of the Indiana Dunes State Park summer playground.

It was also a major block in the path of the approaching Indiana East-West Toll Road!

Now, the park was providing Ted and the Mrs. a fairly good standard of living and he was loath to give it up. He did though, for $750,000.00 from the Toll Road Commission. That may not sound like much loot at the present time, but in today's dollars it would pan out somewhere between two and three million.

So, everybody figured old Ted and his wife would climb into rocking chairs and enjoy their declining years watching the passing scene and lifting themselves out of them only to travel the world.

Ted didn't see this as an option.

After pondering his future for a while he went a half mile east of the original park and purchased a four acre plot at Route 20 and Lake Street in Gary's Miller area. Then he went to work with the zoning board and the city council, got the land zoned for a new bigger and better trailer park and began to build it.

Within six months or so anyone driving by on Route 20, or Lake Street, could see electrical connections and water pipes sticking up about two feet into the air, evenly spaced for the infusion of trailers.

Ted was all set. Ready to roll 'em in.

Enter the legal Mafia.

He received a friendly call from Mayor George Chacharis. An invitation, actually. An invitation for Ted to drop into the Mayor's Office at his leisure for a chat about his proposed new trailer park in the City of Gary.

The mayor and Ted met privately.

I can't tell you what was said.

But I can tell you what both entities in the meeting told me was said. It went something like this:

His Honor: "Well, Ted, I hear you're planning a new park out at Lake Street."

Ted: "Yes siree. Got it all set, papers in order, taxes paid, housing and sewer permits. Gonna be the nicest trailer park in the country."

HH: "Sounds really great, Ted, and the city will be glad to have the addition to the tax base. I sincerely mean that. But, Ted, you've neglected your contribution to the Club Sar and Democratic Party."

Ted: "MY WHAT?"

HH: "Well, you know, party expenses . . ."

Ted: "How much?"

HH: "Comes to $40,000, my good friend."

Ted: "If you think I'm going to give $40,000—just *forget* it! I'm *never going to fork over $40,000* to you or any of your phony horse apple clubs!"

HH: "Then you're *never going to have a trailer park in Gary, you cheap bastard!*"

According to each man the language was slightly more colorful than I would feel comfortable depicting here, but this essentially conveys the heart of the discussion.

For clarity it should be pointed out Mr. Chacharis helped found Club Sar with the words, "We organize today

and in two generations we take the city." The non-political
athletic club was his political base.

Such meetings, in which His Honor's requests were unfulfilled, generally ended with Cha-Cha slamming one of
the ten-foot-tall heavy ornate double doors of his office behind his departing guest with such force the impact could be
heard throughout city hall. This according to several
still-vibrating witnesses was no exception.

Cause and effect. For the next five years motorists were
treated to the sight of a large parcel of land on the northwest
corner of Lake Street and Route 20 with pipes and electrical
connections sticking up in the air for no apparent reason.

Some of those not aware of the city hall stalemate
thought the ground was being prepared for an amusement
park, others that someone was going to open stock pens
there, some that it would be a test field for an industrial ex-
periment and so forth.

Then, one day, the strange assortment of objects were
gone.

The same day, it seemed, when the big new Ted's East
Town Trailer Park, Restaurant and Lounge opened on Route
20 just across the Lake County line in *Porter* County.

No one I know of ever found out what kind of deal Ted
made with the Porter County authorities, but they left him
alone. So much so that ladies of the night were allowed to
openly ply their centuries-old trade there, you could place a
bet on almost anything and, though I don't know if Ted had
a liquor license or not, there was no problem getting a drink
in his large, modern lounge and restaurant.

I do know he never graced the coffers of the Lake
County Demos with $40,000.

The only time I was ever inside the park resulted from a
request I felt I couldn't turn down. Station Assistant Engineer Jim Loupas and I had stopped in a drive-in restaurant

for a quick hamburger and coke on the way back to the station from a remote broadcast at the scene of a Chesterton, Indiana, bank robbery when Gary Detective Captain George Dematroulis snuck up to the car.

"You guys got a minute to do me a favor?" he asked.

Both of us said "Yessir" at the same time.

"Ok," he said. "You see the guy over there in the Cadillac with the two broads?" We agreed to the visual acuity requested.

"He's gonna pull out of here in a couple minutes and I want to know where he's taking the flesh. I can't follow him. He'd spot me in a minute. You think you . . ."

"We got your back," I said. With a quick "Thanks," Dematroulis sidled back to his city car and was sitting innocently in it when the Caddy spun out of the drive-in.

Within seconds I lost him.

He took off south on Liverpool Road at between eighty and ninety miles per hour. Liverpool was a twisting, corkscrew two-lane ribbon of dark asphalt at the time. He had to have known it a hell of lot better than I did.

Jim commented to the effect that he should have been driving; "I would have stayed with him," he said. I mentioned I would rather not end up in the nearby Deep River.

What to do? We didn't want to fail in Dematroulis' request, but the chances of finding the speeding Caddy and its occupants seemed fairly remote. After a short discussion, however, we decided to cruise the neighborhood and see if we could spot the group. At least we could tell the Captain we tried.

So we drove east for a while looking into driveways and at parked cars, even peering into open garages; then north back to Route 20 and finally west back toward Gary and a report of failure. We were approaching Ted's East Town when Loupas, who had climbed into the back seat in order to look out both sides of the car, yelled, "There it is!"

And there it was! Cadillac, man, two women vacating the car and heading into the restaurant-lounge at Ted's.

I parked the Star Chief as far from the entrance as I could, told Jim to sit in the driver's seat with the motor running and transport me out of there if I came running and dove into the car. Sounds kind of over-cautious now, but, at the time, I didn't know what the hell was going down.

No need. No man. No two women. Nothing.

Apparently Mr. Root had designed his facility so you could leave through a back or side or up or down way. They had just vanished.

Still, since I was there, I took a look around. Just imagine a rather large standard bar with a large standard bartender and a large standard bouncer. Sprinkle in a few couples sitting at booths and tables very quietly—at least since the "suit" walked in. I told the bouncer I thought the place was a restaurant. He said, "We can serve you a hamburger." I said, "Thanks, but I'll head on in to Gary," and left.

I described the sortee into the bar to Loupas as we drove back to the drive-in and then repeated it all to Dematroulis.

His "Thanks, guys," ended the adventure. He seemed satisfied just with knowing where the two women had been taken.

I never asked Dematroulis why. It wasn't a news story anyway, just a favor for a friend. Sometimes a good reporter doesn't want to know why. This was one of them.

It came down to the old *quid pro quo*—a favor done, a favor returned—over the years Dematroulis tipped me to a lot of exclusive crime stories.

Maybe touching base with a more seriously motivated Secret Service would brighten your day . . .

A Huge Difference

When President Lyndon Baines Johnson arrived in East Chicago, Indiana, on October 8, 1964 I had been on the scene for two hours.

The first thing I noticed on that chill drizzly morning was the difference between Secret Service security for this Chief Exec compared to that provided for John F. Kennedy during an appearance at McCormack Place in Chicago in 1961 and the sloppy work done in Dallas, Texas, in 1963. This time in the Indiana Harbor section of the Twin City it was huge, transparent and real.

In Chicago, JFK rolled up in an open limo which had been parked unattended for the entire afternoon along Ontario Street at the ABC Vending-Confection Cabinet offices with the usual "show" force of motorcycle escorts, Secret Service agents trotting alongside, dignitaries in the motorcade following—in effect unprotected.

I was not in Dallas, but from the Zapruder film and other sources the inescapable fact presented a picture of a half-hearted protective cover for the President: open windows, people walking around with all sorts of objects in their hands, a torturous parade route and lack of police presence along the way. No, motorcycle cops do not equate to protection.

For Johnson there was a steel curtain.

Walking the five blocks from the cophouse where I had parked to East Chicago Washington High School I counted twenty-seven Secret Service agents. They were easy to spot—when you looked directly at them, they did not look away; the rest of the people walking along the street did. The plainclothes shield was ever present. When I got to the High School Secret Service agents were listening to the fifty telephones set for Press use, one at a time, with a stethoscope. There were no windows open between the Gary Airport where the great man's plane landed and the residential stretch along Grand Avenue leading to the school.

It was as tight as a Texas speed trap.

And then, within sight of the 40,000 people waiting to hear him at the school, the President stopped the motorcade, got out of his enclosed car and charged through the crowd, shaking hands, giving out LBJ pins and, honest to God, kissing babies, to the extreme discomfort of the Secret Service.

Then—this must have seemed the final insult to his guards—he accepted a stranger's invitation to come in and have a cup of coffee. Mrs. Lois Pozywio yelled the invitation to him from her front porch, directly across the street from the school. He moved too quick for the Secret Service to check anything out, but Congressman for life Ray J. Madden, Senator Birch Bayh and County Democrat Chairman Sam Bushemi rode his coattails into the home. The President had two cups of black coffee, distributed pins and finally went back through the crowd to the enclosed grounds and the podium.

He spoke for fifteen minutes (inflated by the national press corps to twenty-five) without saying anything of substance. Two main points: America will be great if we just adhere to the policies of our founders and we must change immigration laws to be less discriminatory.

As for the first point, it was gone when the Supreme Court ruled withholding taxes before people who earned the money even saw it was constitutional, the Civil War and the creation of government-run welfare.

His suggestion was about a hundred years too late and trillions of dollars short.

Since that day in '64 we've sure taken care of his second point.

Thomas J. Knightly and I both got by-lines for coverage of the great man's visit. We agreed the sudden acceptance of the offer of coffee was not a stunt to create some sort of story. Either it was a spontaneous response by Johnson, the Demo officials present and the Secret Service or they should all have been in Hollywood. So we "played" it straight. We made no mention in our combined piece of a possible setup.

Speed was important so our words were fed to the composing room as they were written.

We also quickly concluded the estimate of the crowd's size was inflated, the Secret Service wasted their time and Johnson didn't say a thing even though he was able to quote Franklin Delano Roosevelt, Harry S. Truman, John F. Kennedy and himself.

He said they all agreed about the need for immigration law changes to eliminate discrimination under the present law. I don't remember an explanation of how the then present law discriminated or a mention of how he intended to fix it. The ultimate "fix" down the road a few years was to look the other way.

The Indiana Harbor area of East Chicago had a growing and vocal population of minorities at the time working in the concentrated heavy industry of the region. If any of them told him how to update the immigration laws he kept it a secret.

Maybe he let the cat out of the bag in Indianapolis, his next stop.

Johnson won his only run for the office that year. He was elevated to the presidency by the events in Dallas and refused to run for a second term.

My impression of his term in office was his success in sticking the home base for our space program in Texas. Houston, we have no problem.

And, of course, the complete mishandling of the Vietnam War. Thousands of American kids killed, crippled for life—in many cases physically, others mentally and some both—and the betrayal of a vast number of South Vietnamese who supported us.

It remains the first great meltdown of United States prestige and power. After Vietnam we were known as the country that would "cut and run" when the battle heated up.

From the past flows the future.

Let's leave the official crooks for a look at some real crooks and the way they operate . . .

**Cops and Robbers and Worse . . .
Some Even Elected . . .**

Reform Candidate

There wasn't any place in Lake County, Indiana, where you couldn't participate, engage in, or enjoy a pursuit the law said was illegal. Gambling, prostitutes, drugs, cock fights and so on were readily available. And the citizens were fed up.

Enter Metro Halovachka, the reform candidate for Prosecuting Attorney in 1955.

He promised to clean up. He promised to make the County upstanding, a good place to set up housekeeping, raise a family protected by honest law enforcement, equal justice judges and a healthy environment.

He promised, above all, over and over again, to close the hundreds of little whorehouses from Gary to East Chicago and The Harbor, to Hammond to the Lakefront.

And, when elected and sworn into office, he kept that promise!

He didn't touch gambling, underage drinking, political chicanery or anything mob-connected, but Metro Holovachka closed almost all of the little whorehouses.

And overlooked the opening of one really BIG one.

It was the M. & J. Motel on 25th Avenue, twenty-four blocks west of Broadway. Easy drive from the steel mills in Gary, East Chicago and Indiana Harbor, Standard Oil in Whiting, Air Reduction, Union Tank Car and the rest of the area's heavy industry and their thousands of well-paid male workers plus the occasional school administrator, teacher, government worker and minister of the Gospel.

It was run by Johnny Forman (real name Formosa) at a tidy profit.

After a while Metro loosened the grip a little and slowly the 4 Aces, Chesterfield Club, Venus Café and others re-opened for business, but the M. & J. was still the mother lode.

And this was the stage setting on a Tuesday morning when I entered the newsroom to hear the news phones ringing constantly. Each one, when answered, had a caller telling me there were several Sheriff's cars at the M. & J. around 3 A.M. creating a big ruckus including several shotgun blasts.

The Sheriff's department deputy answering their phone denied having any squad near the M. & J. anytime during the night.

I went with the story anyway.

Just acknowledged the fact that a dozen or so residents of the neighborhood of the M. & J. Motel phoned the station saying there was police action at the M. & J. and shots fired.

The story ran at 6:00, 7:00 and 10:00 A.M. the noon news and then was filed.

The story was no big deal. Police departments of that era in the region did what they pleased and then "wrote" an "official" report to justify their actions.

The *real story was never heard by the public.* It began that evening as I turned the corner into the alley back of the Hotel Gary where my car was parked. A relatively small man dressed in casual work clothes said, "You Gatty Wilson?"

I stopped. Said, "Yes I am. Can I help you?"

"I'ma Tommy Morgano. You no say no more about the M. & J. Motel on the radio."

I said, "What?"

He repeated, "I'ma Tommy Morgano. You don't say about the motel."

And he walked away.

I didn't think much about it. *Disgruntled investor, maybe*, I thought, *or friend of one of the working girls.*

The next morning all that changed significantly.

It was my habit to stop by the cophouse around 5:00 A.M. to look at the overnight reports. I was leafing through them with Sgt. Charley Quade looking over my shoulder when I casually asked, "By the way, Sarge, who's Tommy Morgano?"

Quade actually leaped back about three feet, furtively looked around, then back at me. "Where'd you hear that name?" he whispered.

"Last night. Alley in back of the hotel. He said not to talk about the M. & J."

"Jesus. He's the enforcer for the Outfit, man. He's Acardo's guy in Lake County for Chris' sake."

"They have an interest in the cat house?"

"I don't know," he said, "but if I was you I'd kinda go along with 'im."

Now, by then I had met quite a few policemen in various colored uniforms, titles and so on and was aware that they are no more brave than any other man with a family to feed, bills to pay and a life to live. I had never, however, seen one leap a yard or so backwards just at the mention of a name.

It was no problem for me to figure out I was not being paid enough to take on the Outfit. I never again mentioned the M. & J. on the air.

But, off the air, I still remained curious and one day in the Sands Bar of the Hotel Gary, Jack Leadinghouse pointed out John Forman sitting at the bar. At the time Jack was doing a late night D.J. show and Tony Acardo was one of his sponsors. Acardo had an "office" in a record store in Chicago Heights.

To me this was maybe an opportunity to get a little inside info on the M. & J. At least make the man's acquaintance. I introduced myself and asked if he'd talk to me about his business if I made it "Off the record."

He said, "Seddown, kid. What're you drinken?"

I did, told him any old scotch, neat, would do and said I had heard he was involved with the M. & J.

"Involved? Yeah, I suppose you could say I'm involved with it. You could say I recruit talent." So I asked Johnny how he found his employees that toiled at the Motel. He told me he'd roll up and down Broadway in his gold Caddy convertible and pull into the curb when he saw a "good-looking" girl waiting for transport. He'd politely offer the girl a ride to wherever she was headed. Old John claimed nine out of ten took him up on the offer.

Once underway, he said, he would ask the girl how she would like to make $1,000 to $1,500 per week guaranteed. He told me all of them answered with some form of yes.

"Then," he claimed, "I told them what they'd be doing for the money right up front: on their back, on their stomach, on their knees. I told them the split—their share and the amount for towels, disinfectant, soap, protection, doctor bills—the whole story."

One out of three, he claimed, high school and college students, housewives, clerks, secretaries said "yes" again.

"Don't you have a lot of short-time employees?"

"Not as many as you would think once they see the money," John said. "Like the blacks in the old South, 99 percent of their customers treat them well. For anyone else we have ways of taking care of the problem. We got a few foxes that are part time, but we generally steer them to one of the places in the downtown areas. We're open twenty-four hours seven days every week. Even holidays." He favored me with a chuckle.

Six years later, I did mention the M. & J. again as a brief aside when Tommy Morgano was arrested, in cuffs and waiting to be deported. Tommy had been given the job of opening up the adjacent Porter County and $200,000 to bribe local officials. He offered a deputy Sheriff named Raider $100,000 to be his fixer with the other $100,000 for Raider to buy officials in a position to be helpful to the scheme.

Morgano wanted a gambling house and a brothel in Valparaiso and a second bordello on the lake front. Morgano, in a very menacing voice, assured Raider that he would protect the operations from all competition.

Only hitch was that Raider recorded the entire proposal as they talked things over in Tommy's Caddy and then made the recordings public!

This led to nationwide press coverage, the formation of the Northwest Indiana Crime Commission and a brief public outcry.

It also prodded the Feds into reopening deportation proceedings against Morgano they had started in *1926!*

At the Court deportation hearing, it was testified that Morgano had been personally responsible for the sudden end of almost 300 mobsters during the 40 years Hoover's minions had failed to move. I told the Judge that was a better record against criminals than that of the F.B.I., police and all the rest of the 57,000 law enforcement agencies the taxpayers were shelling out for and we should keep him in the U.S.

The Judge accused me of being "frivolous."

I told his Honor I was very serious. Alas, my appearance was stricken from the hearing record. Morgano was eventually deported. Anthony (Big Tuna) Acardo, the real "Capo de Tuti Capo" of the Chicago Outfit died peacefully in his sleep never having spent a night in jail.

Metro Holovachka did. I never saw him after he left office.

The last time I saw Mr. Formosa was at the grand opening of his home on the lakefront east of Gary. Walking through the house I counted eighteen bedrooms! This was also the last time I saw Frank Sinatra in person. (Or a double so convincing it would fool his mother.)

I don't know if the M. & J. Motel still exists. It's not listed among the area motels in the phone book.

But then, it never was.

Let's go meet the man with three fingers—the friendliest, most likable double-crosser I ever met . . .

Stan "Three Finger" Inkly

Stan Inkly played football for the University of Alabama Crimson Tide, graduated in 1936 and couldn't get a job because he was born with a deformed hand. The index, middle and ring finger of one hand were fused together adding up to one big finger to go with the little finger and thumb. Thus three fingers.

Insurance companies and personnel directors seem about as dumb back then as they are today. Other than the unusual digits, Stan was a horse. Big, hearty handsome fellow with an infectious laugh—just a great guy to be around. But there was no hope of landing a job in mainstream industry with thousands of able-bodied men without noticeable "handicaps" looking for work during the Great Depression. Stan decided he had to start his own business in order to survive.

By the time I met him he owned a huge scrap metal yard in Riverdale, Illinois, and had built a six-floor apartment building on Lyman Avenue across the street from the north end of Harrison Park in Hammond. He and his wife lived on the top floor. He was obviously a successful businessman in scrap metal, investments and the rent from the first to fifth floors didn't hurt the bottom line either.

He was also Hammond's only Republican City Councilman.

Every election time he promised the business community and private citizens of his district less taxes, overpasses to solve railroad delays, public parks, improved bus service and everything else they wanted to hear. Of course he knew none of these things would actually come true. His motions were always voted down 8–1.

So he was seldom heard on the floor of the council except to chide the Democrats about whatever they were planning to fleece the populace, including those in his district.

I met "Three Finger" Inkly as a councilman.

I got to know him after a council session in which several gambling spas had been hit by state and federal authorities in various districts.

After a two-hour discussion which got fairly lively at times, the Demos agreed to ask several owners of such meeting places to cool it until the heat died down. Umm, that wasn't exactly how the legislation went down. It was a resolution requesting the police department to "increase investigative efforts toward discouraging gambling activity," or something like that.

On the way out, Mr. Inkly tapped me on the shoulder and said: "At least there's no gambling in my district, hey kid."

I said: "Stan, I can show gambling going on in your district in at least ten locations in ten minutes."

I thought he'd say something like just playing around with you, or forget it, or no harm, no foul, but his reaction was altogether different.

"You show me *one* place, in the third district just one, and I'll buy you the biggest hamburger in town!"

I folded up my notes, stuck my pen in my pocket, and said: "Get in the car."

I drove to State Street and parked half a block from State Line Avenue in front of the Olympic Billiards. As we got out of the car, I gleefully pointed to the almost century-old bar on the other side of the street and noted it was made famous by the first Mayor Daley of Chicago playing poker there at least once a week, while heading up the Cook County, Illinois Election Board.

Through the double glass doors into the Olympic. When entering you see an oblong room about forty feet deep with a candy counter near the doors and nothing else except for three or four pool tables that are in desperate need of dusting. But when you walk to the rear you uncover a room to your left making the whole area the shape of a backward L. This alcove is equipped with a mirror so those in it can see who is entering the front door.

This Monday night there were seven men sitting at a table laid out for playing barbutte. (Pronounced bar boot)

There was at least $10,000 visible on the table.

Barbutte is a dice game played only for money in which thousands of dollars can change hands in minutes. According to Harold Swaim, then Chief investigator for The Northwest Indiana Crime Commission, there were four winning combinations (6–6, 6–5, 5–5 and 3–3) and four losing pairs (1–1, 1–2, 2–2 and 4–4) and that's the sum of my knowledge about the game.

It was friendly all around: "Hi, Councilman, "Hey, Stan, how's it goin' " all greeted the man.

Back out on the street Inkly stamped a foot two or three times and said: "You know what makes me mad?"

"The unassailable, written in marble, emblazoned on tablets of steel fact that you're going to buy me a hamburger," I ventured.

"No, no," he said. "It's that they didn't have enough respect for me to take the money off the table."

He directed me to Minor-Dunn on Calumet Avenue which was then a restaurant that appeared to date back to the 1800s, when Mr. Hammond opened his slaughterhouse. It had twenty-foot-high ceilings, walls of an indiscriminate color and the odor of old grease. We both had hamburgers the size of dinner plates.

No hamburger ever tasted better.

I wrote the story, and turned it in. The *Hammond Times* never saw fit to print it. For all I know it's still hanging on a hook.

Over the years I found out that Stan was a Republican in name only. Anything he found out his Democrat comrades knew within minutes. He was their foil. If the mayor needed an opposition figure on a blue ribbon committee he would appoint Stan for window dressing. See? Non-partisan.

As an example, while working for WJOB, I had collected more than eighty charges of malfeasance against the officers running the Hammond Fire Department.

Every morning I did a five-minute commentary with these and ended each one with: "Tomorrow, I will speak more about this."

It was driving them crazy. The charges ranged from a ladder truck with a blown motor unrepaired for six months, which resulted in sending firemen in under a steeple during a church fire, to reports of two sets of books, to a new refrigerator in the Chief's home instead of the firehouse for which it was bought, to three men on four-man trucks and on and on.

It was devastating! They had no way of knowing what I was going to hit them with the next morning.

I had met with retired firemen from as far away as Arizona in restaurants in Calumet City, current firemen in my home, even went to the Chief's reward firehouse in Hessville (new one-story homes, little or no business, very little chance of fire) to throw off the spies. I almost received a beating at that Hessville firehouse. Those guys had nothing but gravy and they felt I was threatening their beauty rest.

They tried driving fire engines around the radio station, private threats and calls to the station's ownership. Nothing worked until they sent Assistant Chief Bonar to the firehouses telling the men that if they kept talking to Wilson they would go on extended hours.

That did the trick. My final commentary was to the effect that I would stop the daily shows, since the whole point had been to help the firemen.

But the damage was done. The commentaries forced the mayor, a nice man named Edward Dowling, to name a blue ribbon committee to investigate "Wilson's charges against the Hammond Fire Department."

He named Demo Councilmen Milt Diamond and Mike Matavina and Three Finger Inkly. Diamond, chair. Hey, in that group Inkly's my man, right? So I gave him four pages of charges given to me by firemen past and present the afternoon before the evening hearing.

When I entered the conference room there were present Chief Edward Spolnik, three assistant chiefs including John Bonar, who had carried the threat of extended hours to the firehouses, seven other officers and one lone fireman sitting by himself in the back of the room. There was also the woman who kept the books for the fire department and was seething over my program examining the points I had been told about there being two sets of books for the department expenditures.

A few minutes after Diamond gavelled the August body to order, Spolnik testified he had made no threat of extended hours for the men of the department. I asked Assistant Chief Bonar why he still had a job. He said, "What do you mean?"

I said, "If I misquoted my boss that badly I'd be selling beer at ballgames."

At that point Diamond ruled I was not a part of the hearing and I could remain silent and stay or be escorted from the room. I stayed. An hour later the committee ruled there was no validity to the charges I had broadcast.

My man Inkly had never opened his mouth.

The next morning I reported the committee's findings.

Later that day I asked Inkly why he had not brought up any of the additional charges I had given him. "Oh," he said, "I lost them."

At that moment I realized that Democrat, Republican, Environmentalist, Socialist, Communist are simply meaningless *labels*. The *category* is politician. And no politician is going to do anything to embarrass another politician unless that person could undermine his or her own graft. Same goes for police, judges, schoolteachers, doctors, prostitutes, ministers—each is a closed entity when it comes to trouble. Regardless of the label they will do all they can to protect their category. This made me a lot harder to fool. Thank you, Stan!

Eight months later Spolnik was quietly replaced as Chief.

Eighteen *years* later, after a seven-year hitch as Manager of Press Relations with the Northern Indiana Public Service Company and a second go around with the *Times*, I returned to WJOB and had the most popular morning drive-time radio program in Northwest Indiana. It was rated eighteenth in the sixty-plus station Chicagoland area. This is still the only time in the station's history it made the top twenty.

As fate or the great quantum field or God decreed, Inkly, getting back into politics after a long period of retirement, came to the station to record some paid appeals for votes.

On his way out he stopped by my office and asked me to slip in a good word on the air for his run. I told him I had orders to stay strictly neutral, but privately wondered if the man had lost touch with reality. I said nothing to his benefit on the air.

He lost.

You could take it that I was partly to blame for his failure or that I was not the only person that had found him untrustworthy. He was a great guy to pal around with, but you wouldn't want to give him the key to your cookie jar.

What goes around comes around almost always.

Whatever the reason, sheer coincidence, a higher power, quantum physics—these completed loops happened time after time as I wondered through the people's world as a reporter.

In many cases the odds were unbelievable, but they happened.

Follow me in an excursion into the numbers racket and just one of my arguments with an "official" police report . . .

Black Gold

The Lucky Strike Policy Wheel was run out of a drug store in the 1700 block of Gary's main north south thoroughfare by Hutchen Upshaw. Broadway, as it is still called, split the African-American midtown community in half from 10th Avenue to 25th Avenue. At 10th Avenue railroad tracks signaled the crossover from white downtown Gary north to Number One Broadway and the main entrance to U.S. Steel Corporation's five-mile-long Gary Steel Works. At 25th Avenue housing stopped for ten blocks for Gleason Park. Gary's Glen Park area started on the south side of 35th. The midtown areas extended to the east and west of Broadway for a dozen or so blocks in each direction.

If you entered the Upshaw drug store you would notice what seemed to be an ordinary glass door about halfway down the store's depth on your right. It wasn't until someone opened the door for you that you could see the glass was about 3 inches thick.

The door was always locked because it opened on a flight of stairs that led to the second floor living quarters of Hutch, his wife Ardenia, teenage daughter, and the family's maid.

It also held the take of the Lucky Strike wheel in a very large safe.

On the particular morning of this incident—shortly after 10:30—one of three men pressed the pearl button that told the residents in the living quarters upstairs someone wanted to gain entrance. Mrs. Upshaw answered and when the three men flashed what seemed to her to be genuine FBI credentials, she let them in.

Five minutes later Mrs. Upshaw, her daughter and the maid were trussed up like steers to be branded and laying face down on the living room carpet, according to their sworn statements.

One of the intruders explained to Mrs. Upshaw that she could either reveal the combination that opened the safe or she could watch her maid say goodbye to the good life forever. And if she was reluctant, her daughter would be next in line.

Mrs. Upshaw complied.

Less than five minutes later the vault door was opened, the money gone and so were the three guests. That morning the armed bandits had gotten the winning numbers.

A little over an hour later Hutch trudged up the stairs and found his womenfolk tethered, gagged and uncomfortable. He said later he was concerned more for their safety than by the open door of the safe.

This I will not dispute, but a lot of lifestyles were enhanced by payoffs from that lockbox.

Once informed, it took only seconds for police radios to start squawking about a ten-thirty-six at Upshaw's drugstore. The open safe mutely testified to the crime with its empty interior. If you ever desire to see a concentration of working police you have to be on hand when somebody hits one of their payoff places. So I had no trouble imagining the crowd when I dialed Hutch's private line. He answered on the first ring and seemed relieved it was me. In answer to my "What the hell's going on at your digs, Hutch?" he told me the information you've just read. I asked him how the ladies were and he said shaken up a little, but otherwise undamaged. My next question was how much the robbers got.

"They got it alllll," he moaned, "thutty-foe thousand, six hunnert and foety-two dollas."

I led with the story on the noon news—one of three fifteen-minute Covering Calumet newscasts carried by the station and the reason I could not personally go to the scene. As I left the broadcast studio I could hear the newsroom phone ringing.

"This is Captain Curley," the voice on the phone said as I picked it up. "You got the take all wrong on that Lucky Strike story. They got three hundred and forty-six dollars!"

"Hello," I answered. "Tim, be serious. Hutch carries that much in his watch pocket. He personally gave me the amount I used."

"Well, you can use any amount you want, but our official report is gonna carry the three hundred plus."

The next day in their endlessly timid way the *Post-Tribune* sort of backed me up by running a two column headline $34,642 or $346 with a full column two-inch-high question mark.

The original figure was, of course, correct. Hutch, under stress, had given me the previous day's gross take of the wheel. Nobody, not the mayor, courts, police, or anyone else, wanted that figure out on the street. It probably shook up payoff amounts from the county courthouse to city hall and the police station.

I carried the true amount on the 6:15 P.M. Covering Calumet and then dropped it. They must have smoothed everything out as far as the payoffs were concerned. I heard no more about it.

As far as I could determine, no one was ever arrested for the heist. And no official ever commented further on it . . . at least not to me. The nickels, dimes and quarters continued to pour in. The wheel kept running.

Now the policy, or numbers game, is run by the states so

all the government agencies get a legal bit of the pie. Not illegal anymore. Hell, it's called a state lottery, encouraged and advertised on TV.

That's progress in the good old land of the free. What's next? Dog fights?

The swiftest and most massive responses by police I witnessed as a reporter other than for show (parades, presidential motorcades, tribute to a fallen officer, etc.) was in response for a crime committed by one of their own, a crime or trouble involving someone who was paying them off or a complaint by the mob that *they* were being ripped off.

Sad, but true.

Sixteen cars showed up near Washington Park Race Track to take down two men who had rented a second floor room and were past-posting the races and cutting into the Outfit's profits. There were seven Gary cars on the scene within minutes when the owner of a garage, driving dead drunk demolished two cars waiting to make a left turn at Route 20 and Old Gleason Road. He had been paying off for towing jobs for years. Lots and lots of cars turned up when a rookie cop called for backup where four men were removing tires from a boxcar in a stopped train. The four turned out to be fellow officers. As I remember the four offenders were punished with time off with pay.

Before you lean too heavily on them just remember lawyers protect fellow lawyers, doctors cover the mistakes of other doctors, politicians—well we all know about politicians.

A reporter can cripple his, or her, future by telling the truth. Most of the time the house he works for won't print or air the item if it hurts an advertiser, friend of the owners or senior editors; or similar reasons. But even if they do the reporter is sure to lose the person as a source and all of the person's friends and colleagues.

Ask Connie Chung.

A reporter without contacts is as helpless as a cat without claws.

So don't look at the mass media for truth, especially if they're quoting an "official" report or quoting an "official spokesman" or a prepared story handed out by anybody.

You must read it, determine who benefits by what is said, and then use the brain you come equipped with to analyze it.

Unless you enjoy being whipped back and forth by the daily dose of propaganda.

Sometimes individuals are more deadly . . . including females . . .

The program cover and tier pass for President John F. Kennedy's only speech outside of Washington, D.C., in 1961.

Wilson, left, and Lee Cohn at Bethlehem Steel groundbreaking.

Gary Mayor Peter Mandich, center, announces for Sheriff's office. East Chicago Mayor, Walter Jeorse, endorses and mugs for the camera.

Ahhh, show biz! Wilson and Bill Gains wait for election returns at 3 A.M.

No. NO! The *elephant* is Bimbo, the girl, Heather Spelling, of London, United Kingdom. It's circus time in the Sam Miller operated Hammond Civic Center.

General Stephan Holmes, 5th Army, presents awards for radio campaign to recipients Wilson (left) and Roy Tobin of local FM station.

The Kentucky Rifle

Opal Collins was just simply too beautiful. She had the figure of a young Monroe, the face of an angel, and the smile of the most gorgeous, friendly girl in your high school.

She also had the mind of a timber wolf.

This, up until a summer day in the Hessville area of Hammond, Indiana, was betrayed, I was told, only by her eyes. Looking into those eyes was looking at bone-chilling cold. They were not responsive to any emotion, without the slightest hint of pity and that was when she was feeling kind. I found them so lightly blue as to be almost colorless which added to the impression of lack of warmth.

Of course when I first looked into them she had fifteen minutes earlier shot a .22 rifle at five members of her immediate family seventeen times and twelve of the bullets were fatal. She disposed of her paraplegic former soldier husband, his two teenage sisters and their mother on a Sunday afternoon. Her only "miss" was a head-high notch in the frame of a doorway her husband's eight-year-old brother dashed through. Had he been half a step slower it would have been thirteen out of seventeen and five dead.

I was in the middle of a two-year sentence working for the first of three consecutive certifiably insane radio station owners and, since radio news is immediate, was called to do a live report.

When I reached the scene Opal was leaning against the white front wall of the one-story frame house looking at the police activity swirling around her with detachment—as though she was a gal out for a stroll and just stumbled onto the area of slaughter. She was not in cuffs, but somebody had taken the rifle away from her. Within ten feet to her left, sitting in a rocking chair on a foot-high raised open porch was the father—called home from the mill to find his family gone.

He wasn't rocking. Just staring straight ahead.

I stuck a microphone in front of Opal and asked if she was Opal Collins. She just looked through me. I asked if she could hear me. Not even a flicker of movement. I asked if she had shot members of her family. This time there was the slightest tilt of her head. Since a nod doesn't do a radio reporter much good, I asked again. Her face reflected boredom, so I asked *why* she did it.

At first I thought she was going to ignore that question as she had the others; then, in a soft southern accent she said, "They gave me a rough time, so I killed the sons of bitches."

Back in those late 1950s days, that answer didn't do much for a radio reporter either, even as a quote!

A uniform officer came and took her away. Led her would be a more accurate description. She went quietly, still uncuffed.

When I asked the father if he would like to make a comment for local radio he looked up at me like I was absolutely insane. No sound bites from the family so I turned to the police spokesman for a brief description of the sequence of events. Even the investigators were not sure of how things went down that early in their investigation.

However, I was told the Collins family, mother and the two sons and daughters, had recently moved to Hammond from Kentucky following the father who had been employed at a local steel mill. Opal had apparently been intentionally left behind, but insisted on joining them later. This intelligence apparently volunteered by neighbors.

Since Sunday afternoon was the only time off I had, I recorded the basic story for broadcast, wrote a couple of short takes for the overnight announcing staff, relayed the information to United Press International and went home.

In small-time radio you were given a meaningless title taking you out of the hour and wage laws allowing the owner to work you eighty or ninety hours a week for a very small salary. My workday began at 5 A.M. at the police station reviewing overnight reports and could end at midnight following a city council or school board meeting. I was also on call for any major fire, "name murder" or other unusual reportable event.

I was the "News Director."

The next morning during that 5 A.M. tour of the police station I stopped by Opal's cell. She was standing behind the bars of her cell door in the basement lockup located in the Hammond City Hall. I asked her if she was ok. She said, "They're all alright, aren't they?" A nearby turnkey said it was the first sympathetic words he had heard her speak.

A few months later Opal was convicted, sentenced to die and transferred to the Lake County Jail in Crown Point some thirty miles south of Hammond. The first multiple person jailbreak from the venerable institution occurred about a month later and there were two more within the next three weeks!

This was unusual even for the ancient lockup made famous by the gun totin' bank robber John Dillinger and there was much speculation as to why this was suddenly occurring. Age of the building? Insufficient personnel? A canny prisoner planning the escapes?

None of the above. A deputy finally told me—after some prompting—that it was Opal's actions that paved the way for the rash of flights to freedom. Seems she had figured out the State of Indiana would not execute a woman carrying a child. So, at the 3 A.M. cell checks she was offering her naked body to the officers. The deputy claimed she was so hard to resist that they discontinued the early morning rounds of inspections. The jailed prisoners were free to figure exit strategies and be missing by the daylight roll call. This sequence of events was not published at the time! Nor has it been until now, as far as I know. They put a curtain over her cell and cotton in their ears, resumed the cell checks and the jailbreaks stopped.

Since that ploy didn't work out Opal got religion. Praying to a newfound savior and swearing she was a changed woman. She shed this dodge when she was told Indiana Governor Harold Handley had commuted her sentence to life in prison. The Governor marked his largess with the words, "No woman has been executed in the history of Indiana and the first will not be while I'm Governor."

I was told that two weeks after arriving at the Indiana State Women's Prison Opal gave the warden a glass of water with slivers of glass in it. This, too, was kept from the general public.

I don't know if it's true, but the report didn't surprise me and the source was reliable and on the scene.

Oh, yes. Why did she do it? The official version was that she wanted her husband to give her his $10,000 government insurance settlement and he refused. Trial testimony was that she badly mistreated the chair-bound man back in Kentucky and that at least a part of the reason for moving the family to Hammond had been to distance themselves from her. Still, they must not have known her true tenacity in seeking the money and surely not her accuracy with a light rifle. Both incredibly costly errors!

She stands as the most deadly person I ever met.

Poor George did half as much damage as Opal, and he didn't even have half the mind . . .

George Robert Brown

A third-grade boy taking a shortcut through a vacant lot on his way home from school was the first to notice the girl's arm sticking up out of the sand in an unincorporated area of Lake County near East Gary (now New Chicago).

The first adults the boy told about the unusual sight ordered him to go wash his face and quit making things like that up. When the boy refused to admit to a hoax, his father accompanied him to the spot.

Within two hours the Sheriff's department had exhumed the body of a fifteen-year-old New Chicago schoolgirl named Lana Brock.

She was partially clothed, had been beaten and apparently sexually molested.

Chief Investigator Sandor Singer of the Sheriff's Department or the Prosecutor's Office became the spokesman for the case and my source of choice. I was never really sure what hat Sandor was wearing at a given time, so I called him Chief Spokesman for the Prosecutor's Office.

Within the next forty-eight hours twenty-six-year-old Glen Park Beauty Parlor owner Mildred Grigonis had been reported missing, and I was becoming a real pain in a sore place to Sandor Singer. Her car had been found abandoned on a street near New Chicago—east of Glen Park—and I had talked to enough people in the neighborhood to become convinced that Lana Brock's father should be hauled into the Sheriff's office and questioned. At least as a "person of interest."

Sandor wasn't having it.

About all he would say was along the lines of "Let's give this a little time to simmer. I haven't got anything to question him about."

But the girl's father was known in his neighborhood as a ne'er-do-well, a man who was often in his cups and heavy-handed when it came to disciplining his children. Both females were closely tied to the vicinity of the Brock home and there was obvious foul play surrounding the two. Grigonis' car exhibited signs indicating it had not been voluntarily left by its driver. All this seemed mighty suspicious to me and pointed to Mr. Brock.

In the meantime, over in the detectives bullpen at the Gary police station, Kappas and Sanders must have been on Chief Foley's short list for some reason. I say this because they had been given the chore of hunting down a man named George Robert Brown in connection with a series of very minor traffic offenses. Generally police detectives are not assigned to minor traffic violations, but anyway, it was a job and they were on it.

The thorough duo called the Brown household for a few days requesting each time that his wife, the only person who ever answered the phone when the two called, to please ask her husband to drop into the cophouse and square up the traffic tickets. "I sure will," she would assure them.

Well, after about a half dozen such conversations the team decided to ask Mrs. Brown to come to the station in person and clear the matter up (pay the fines). She showed up complete with baby, was greeted courteously by our investigators and shown the seat of honor at their desk in the squad room.

"We asked you down here, Mrs. Brown, because your husband won't come talk to us and we can't understand why," Kappas told her.

"Maybe," she replied with a smile, "it's because *of the two women he killed.*"

Sanders later told me it seemed to take him forever to get his mouth closed and, when he looked over at him, Kappas was apparently having the same problem.

"What two women???" they asked in unison when they got their breath back.

"Oh, you know," she said, "that young girl in the sand and the beauty-shop girl from Gary."

She was in the course of events introduced to Sandor by the two detectives and with her guidance he was able to dig up Grigonis' ID, driver's license, credit cards and some personal items from where they had been buried in the Brown's backyard. This led to George Robert's arrest and he, in turn, led them to where he had dumped Mildred Grigonis' body in the ditch at the foot of the runway at King's Sky Ranch Airport. He had been dumping garbage and trash from his house on her body for the six weeks, or so, since her murder.

The scene was surreal.

You couldn't help being reminded of an old-time horror movie, expecting to see Frankenstein's monster or the Wolf Man pop out of the shadows.

There were searchlights, dozens of police cars with bubble lights spinning, backhoes, front loaders, dump trucks and a waiting ambulance. The ditch at the foot of King's airport runway was about fifteen feet deep and twenty feet wide stretching the width of the runway itself and slightly beyond from what I could see outside the glare of the floodlights.

The ditch had apparently become a dumping site for trash from a lot of that area's homes and businesses. This is where Mr. Brown said he had dumped Grigonis' body and the authorities were at work trying to uncover it.

They did. A deputy yelled, "She's here!"

The ambulance took her to the morgue in one of the

hospitals. The Coroner's Office would later use this case as a reason for a lab and morgue of their own. Nothing is wasted politically. I seem to remember they got it.

My memory says George got life with no parole because of his mental lack and cooperative stance with investigators. He and his wife Helen had met, fallen in love, and were married while residents of the mental hospital at Westville, Indiana. There was testimony that he had very limited mental capacity. He had the mind of a six-year-old.

Three footnotes to this yarn—back in the newsroom we used to call them sidebars:

A roommate of Brown told me that George had bragged about breaking out of Westville one night, thumbing a ride into Gary and splitting a man's head open "like a watermelon." The only instance I could remember that fit the description was the death of a dairy company night watchman who had been found one Sunday morning with his head split open "like a watermelon." Sergeant Charley Quade chased me out of the record room when I tried to line up possible dates for a story.

Back then Gary police records—paid for by the taxpayers—were very confidential to cover up lies, mistakes and incompetence. We'll never know. Maybe now with the Freedom of Information Act, someone who cared could take a look, but they would probably find the report altered, exempted or destroyed.

Mildred Grigonis was carrying $640 from the beauty shop the evening she went missing. The next day George Robert bought a used car for $640.

The autopsy showed sand in Lana Brock's lungs.

The fifteen-year-old schoolgirl had been buried alive.

George Robert was, apparently, driven to crime by a combination of sexual desire and lack of any way to make an honest dollar. Let's stay on the police beat for a story that points out another forceful motive to break the law . . . re-venge.

Redheads Trigger Heat

When we first moved to Gary from Ashtabula, Ohio, we settled into an apartment on Juniper and Lake Streets in the Miller area of the city between Lake Michigan and the Lagoon.

That explains why I was driving west on Fifth Avenue (Route 20) in the pre-dawn hours of a Tuesday morning.

Ordinarily I would turn south on Broadway and go to the cophouse at 10th Street to look through the overnight police reports. This morning, however, once I made the left arc where Route 20 becomes Gary's 5th Avenue I could see the huddle of bubble lights on the west side of Broadway from twelve blocks away.

As I coasted to a stop the view was of tired firemen rolling up hoses and collecting fire axes and other tools of their trade after an hours-long battle of some intensity.

A quick peek through the shattered glass door showed me the entire interior of the Lighthouse Restaurant was blackened heaps of debris.

I went in search of a white helmet.

When I spotted an officer's helmet, I walked over to him, introduced myself as the new reporter for WWCA News and asked the usual string of questions—all your people ok? any civilians hurt or killed? what time did you get the call? how many trucks? owner on the scene? and so on. All went well until I asked if he had any idea what caused the fire. He looked at me like I was kidding with him, saw I was serious and jerked a thumb toward the glassless former picture window of the restaurant.

"What are you blind?" he asked in apparent awe.

Sitting, lined up like soldiers at attention for the whole world to see were four blackened ten-gallon milk cans!

"Umm, gasoline?" I asked.

"Smells like it to me," he said and turned back to loading equipment onto a nearby rig.

Cans of gasoline thrown through a window suggested arson.

This began a cascade of public guessing over who might have started the blaze. Union beer haulers were threatening a strike. Could they be the culprits? Maybe the owner had forgotten the obligatory gratuity to the Outfit. Or the city. Or the politicos, etc.

Three days later around 9:30 A.M. I decided to get off that tack which was going nowhere and find out if the owner was going to rebuild. It was as easy as looking up the number in the phone book and dialing it.

But I was disappointed when the man's wife answered the phone.

"Sorry to bother you," I said identifying myself. "I was going to ask your husband if he would rebuild the restaurant."

"I don't give a good bleep bleep what the son of a bleep does with his bleeping restaurant," she said with a teaspoon of disgust overlaying a thinly veiled pinch of anger. "Bleep him and his bleeping whore."

"Uh huh," I cleverly replied, then; "You sound like you didn't much care for the restaurant."

"Not the restaurant, you bleep," she said making me feel as though I was one of the family. "I told him if he didn't stop bleeping that bleeping redhead I would burn his bleeping business down."

I didn't have to look up the number to call Police Chief John Foley. That one was memorized.

"Chief, do you have reason to believe the Lighthouse Restaurant was torched for personal reasons?"

"We certainly do," he said.

I wrote the story, but sat on it through the 10:00 and 11:00 A.M. newscasts. I wanted to be sure the *Gary Post-Tribune's* absolute deadline had passed. Once the presses were rolling I knew they couldn't steal it.

I opened the noon Covering Calumet news with the words: "Good afternoon. The award-winning WWCA news department has learned exclusively from reliable sources and Gary Police Chief John Foley that the Lighthouse Restaurant fire was set for personal reasons . . ."

Chief Foley told me the next day that as soon as he heard me say "personal reasons" he looked at the sweep of the second hand of his office clock and that four seconds later his phone rang.

"Is what that radio reporter Wilson is saying true?" The question was posed by James Rasmussen, Managing Editor of the *Post-Tribune.*

Foley said he told him I had it right.

"Did you confirm it for him?"

"I certainly did," the Chief said.

"Well, why the hell didn't you tell my reporters?" Rasmussen asked with force. Foley told me he sounded like his fingers were about to crush the telephone.

Foley told me he told him: "Your reporters didn't ask."

As an aside, one time United Press International Indianapolis Bureau Chief Jep Cadou told me this story hooked me on as a stringer for UPI. I felt I should have shared it with the Yellow Pages, the owner's wife and Chief Foley.

It also began a long running feud between me and Rasmussen which he had no hope of winning. He had the larger staff, but I had a deadline every second 24/7. There was nothing he could do to catch up once his paper "went to sleep" after its absolute deadline except run an extra or stop the presses—both money-losing choices.

Sometimes there's a very personal fire—in the belly.

Illegal Care

It would usually begin something like this: a folded piece of paper laying on the news desk. Unfolded, it would usually carry some version of, "I'm PG. Can you help me?"

In the 1960s a good news reporter was supposed to know everything, have contacts in all layers of society and be able to arrange anything. And I could. At one time I had more than 300 unlisted numbers (with addresses).

There was never a signature.

It didn't matter. Contact was sure to be made.

Sometime later in a hallway, cloakroom, office or parking lot a female would walk up and say, "Did you get my note?"

"Something about needing help?" I'd ask just to be sure. The reply was "Yes" or a nod or a beseeching look.

My answer never varied. "I will help put you in touch with the syndicate doctor—no one else. You convince him you're legit—not from the police—and you will be taken care of by a doctor in a medical setting without undue risk, pain or cost. It's a standard fee. I will not give you the name of a kitchen scraper or closet midwife or anybody else. Ok?"

Answers varied from "What happens?" to "How much does it cost?"

The fee back then was $750 plus the cost of getting to and from and the charge for an overnight hotel room if the girl did not want to return home after the first procedure. It was a two-day deal. The first day the doc would pack the womb with antibiotics and loosen the fetus. The second day he would remove it. While his main job was with connected ladies of the night and girlfriends and friends of the mob, he did take "outside" patients if he was very sure he was not being entrapped.

Now you may wonder why I would be involved in aiding and abetting a felony. The reason is I knew one thing as an absolute. Once a girl clamped her jaw shut and decided on an abortion there was nothing I knew of that could stop her from having it done or attempting it herself. I had witnessed too many botched abortions brought to area hospitals and morgues to just say "no" and let the girl jeopardize herself now or in the future from the torn up results of an amateur attempt. One girl went to a tabletop practitioner near Northwestern University and bled through fourteen towels while being driven home. She survived, but has had no babies.

I had offered the girl's friend an attempt to get the Outfit doc, but he said the woman up near the university would do it for a third of the price. When he called after the trip and identified himself I kidded him with, "Why are you calling? To borrow a shovel?"

He said, "That's not funny" and told me of the bleeding.

So, when asked, I would make the call.

In an hour or two there would be a phone call wanting the girl's name and a phone where she could be reached. That's all.

I was never privy to what the patient was asked when she was contacted. I imagined general health questions, how she happened to be needing the doctor's attention and whether or not she could pony up the required $750. Big pay in the 1960s.

Because of one such incident in the early '60s I can provide some details. One girl told me she was to be at a certain drug store in Chicago at a given time and to wait there until contacted. She told me this because she wanted me to drive her there.

I refused, but she said she couldn't tell her husband and she had no friends she trusted enough not to blab the thing all over town. It should be noted she already had several children and did not want another under any circumstance. It was the one and only time I went along with the "patient."

Actually she drove to the drugstore. We waited about ten minutes—time for a cup of coffee—when a man slid into the booth next to me.

"You the one waiting for the Doc?" he asked her.

With her nod he said, "Follow me" and got up. We followed and he led us to a corner office in a high rise across the street. We arrived in time to watch the doctor get a hug, kiss and "Thanks again, Doc" from one of his regular customers.

When he noticed me he said, "What the hell are you doing here?"

"Whoa," I said, "I just accompanied the lady . . ."

"Well you're not supposed to be in this office." Then after a brief pause he added, "Well, since you're here sit down over there and wait."

He took her into an adjoining room and brought her out a few minutes later. She looked a bit pale, but otherwise in no trouble.

She drove us back to the Calumet area saying her hubby would be suspicious if she were to be away overnight.

The next day she drove to the office. I drove us home with a little bit of a scare on the way. Rolling south along the Outer Drive near downtown Chicago there was suddenly hundreds, it seemed, of police sirens in back of us! *Jesus*, I thought as I pulled to the curb, *they've got me. I'll spend the rest of my life in jail!"*

But the police cars and cycles swept on by us. It was a motorcade for Presidential candidate Richard Nixon!

I drove her to the radio station where my car was parked, got in my car and drove home in fine shape, feeling satisfied with the procedure, the escape and knowing a burden had been lifted from a friend.

An hour later I was lying on the couch shaking all over with delayed shock. This happened to me two other times: once several minutes after leaning into a curve on a motorcycle coming out of Columbus, Ohio, and going across two lanes of oncoming traffic before righting the machine and once when a railroad crossing gate malfunctioned and came down like a giant knife hitting the hood of the convertible right in front of my face.

"Serves you right. You shouldn't get mixed up in such things," said my marvelous wife. The only person who has heard or been aware of this story except the participants until this writing.

At one time, alcohol, gold and gambling were illegal. Illegality did not eliminate alcohol, gold or gambling. It has also not eliminated habit-forming drugs, smuggling money out of the U.S. or stopping undocumented people from crossing our borders. Such laws, however, have made lots of money for lawyers, judges, policemen, prison guards, prison builders, rehabilitated criminals now telling people not to do what they did, counselors, psychiatrists, doctors, staffers of Alcoholics Anonymous, Gamblers Anonymous and Columbian officials.

All honorable people on the right side of the law.

For a long time "leaders" made money lobbying to make abortions legal. Now a lot of people are making money lobbying to make it illegal again.

Maybe that's why all these problems of society are kept alive.

Still, I do not recommend actions that lead to delayed shock.

Want to know how easy a reporter's life can be? Follow me.

Popesque, Po and Skinta

For eleven months of the year Popesque was the tricycle cop in downtown, Gary, Indiana. As far as I could tell Popesque didn't have a first name. Everybody, including his fellow officers, just called him Popesque.

His duties included touring the parking meter streets and writing tickets if the meter had expired and marking the outside rear tires with chalk on the end of a stick. Even if the meter had been "fed" when he made his rounds an hour and a half later, if the chalk mark still showed the vehicle would be ticketed. He would also smooth over small disturbances, take a report of a fender bender and call for backup for anything serious.

The twelfth month he drove a medium-sized truck in the downtown area and collected "donated" Christmas gifts for his fellow officers and the clerks and other police department employees. A policeman or woman could request a pen and pencil set, a small radio, maybe a sweater; a sergeant a small TV or easy chair, topcoat maybe, detectives a color TV or bicycle for a kid and so on up the ladder to a bedroom set or something of that value for the Chief.

Popesque seemed content.

On this particular day, I was not so happy.

My car was equipped with a transmitter for remote broadcasts, microphones, tape decks and the rest of the necessary equipment for a live report of a fire, shooting, auto accident with injuries, ground breaking, or anything else of note. To do anybody any good the car had to be close to the

Hotel Gary where the radio station studios (and me) were located.

Now, I could not do hourly newscasts, cover the news, write the news, clear the wire service machines and go out every hour, feed a parking meter and roll the car a quarter wheel turn to hide the chalk mark.

So, Gary Police Chief John Foley worked out a plan where I could park in the alley in back of the hotel even though cars parked there would ordinarily be ticketed. Since, he said, he couldn't tell 150 cops of the arrangement if I was ticketed, I was to leave it on the windshield, put it in the glove compartment overnight and put it *back* on the windshield the next day so passersby and cops would think the car had already been properly ticketed.

Popesque was, of course, informed of the arrangement.

Dandy. Car handy. No problem.

Enter Sergeant Po. Actual name Poherelic.

I pull into the alley after covering the awarding of a new car to a contest winner and a marked patrol car is idling there. The arm resting on the passenger side windowsill is covered with Sergeant's stripes so I figure he's in the know. I park, put the parking ticket under the windshield wiper blade and head for the studios.

When I get to the corner of the hotel I glance back and notice the Sergeant now has a boot on my back bumper and is writing a ticket.

Trotting back to the car I say, "Hi, Sarge, what gives?"

He says, "What the hell you think you're doing? Make us look like idiots?"

"Whoa, Sarge," I say. "We have an arrangement so I can park here and have access to the car for radio reports."

He finishes writing the ticket, tears it off his pad and says: "This car's parked here an hour from now when I get back it gets towed!"

I hold out my hand for the ticket. He whooshes it away, stalks around me and the car and slaps it on the windshield over the one I had put there.

By now, I'm seething. This idiot is going to make my job harder by a factor of four or five. He put it there, I left it there, got in the car and headed down the alley on my way to the cophouse. When I reached the intersecting east-west alley Popesque turned the corner on his tricycle, jumped off and stood in front of my car.

"Jesus, Wilson, don't drive around town with the god-damn tickets on your windshield. I know you got a ok on parking, but don't make us look silly."

"Alright," I sighed, "gimme the tickets."

He handed me the tickets and I continued on to the cophouse.

I was steaming down the hall toward the Chief's office when Sergeant John Skinta stopped me.

"Where ya goin', Wilson?" he asked.

"I gotta see the Chief," I answered, stepping to go around him.

He reached out both arms, took me by the shoulders and squared me up in front of him.

"Tell me," he said.

"I'll tell Chief Foley," I said, trying again to go around him.

"Tell *me*," he repeated, squaring me up in front of him again.

Now I'm 6'2" and not that easy to do that sort of thing to on an everyday basis, but Skinta was between 6'7" and 6'8" and had no trouble.

"Dammit, Sarge," I finally said, "A sergeant on your force threatened to have my car towed if I park in back of the hotel anymore and at a hundred and eight-fifty a week I can't afford to be paying towing charges for parking where you guys told me to park."

"What the hell sergeant?" Skinta asked.

I looked at the ticket. "A Sergeant Po," I said.

"Oh, Christ," Skinta said. "Not Po again. Go park your car where it belongs and I'll take care of Po."

"I don't know, John," I said, "this cat Po seemed damned determined to get my car out of there."

"Go back," Skinta said. "Park your car. It'll be alright."

"Well, ok. But towing fees come out of my kids' food," I said, beginning to turn back.

The voice came from out of nowhere.

"One little complaint and you go running to mama, right?

"Now what the hell is *this* all about?" Skinta said, looking like his patience was stretched to the limit.

I looked over my shoulder and it was Popesque thinking I had gone to Skinta complaining about him yanking the parking tickets off my windshield.

I had never mentioned Popesque to Skinta.

I waved to them both and left it up to Skinta to bring the beat cop up to speed.

With some fear I parked my car back in the alley. At 6:45 that evening it was still there, untowed. I never ran across Sergeant Poherlic again.

Later a cop told me the brother of one of the other sergeants was killed during an armed robbery in progress while his on duty Sergeant Po was selling used cars.

His fellow officers had no trouble controlling Sergeant Po.

As a sidebar, Popesque was prominent in a very unusual incident in my life. My wife, Joyce, and I traveled to Indianapolis to visit and spend the night with friends who had moved there from Gary.

I dreamed in full color for only the second time in my

life. The dream took me back to Gary and I was driving my wife downtown for shopping on my way to work. As she got out of the car and started across Broadway she was hit by a bus. The bus was green up to the windows and yellow from there across the top. I frantically parked the car somehow, raced to the scene and Popesque was already there bending over her. He looked up at me with great sadness and said, "She's gone, Gary."

That straightened me upright in bed with a panicky sick feeling. Rather like being hit in the stomach with a baseball bat.

After calming down a little, I debated waking my wife up and telling her about the dream. Then, I thought, it's just a dream, so I rolled over and went back to sleep.

And the same dream in full color unfolded before me like watching a rerun of a movie. Everything was authentic except the color of the bus! Popesque, the buildings at 5th and Broadway, people, background. And it was exactly the same dream, scene by scene, second by second. It's the only time anything like this had ever happened to me. Now I'm really shook.

This time I woke Joyce up and told her about it.

My incredible, practical lady said, "It's just a dream. Go back to sleep, sweetheart."

I never to my knowledge saw a green and yellow bus in Gary. If Joyce ever saw one anywhere, she was wise enough not to mention it to me.

My wife, after great doctors gave her six years to live with scleroderma, lived *thirty-six* years and died in an emergency room while the "doctor" was waiting for test results.

The other dream in color?

At the age of six and very hungry in the middle of the Great Depression, I dreamed of a giant strawberry ice cream cone. It was perfect! Big rounded ball of ice cream atop a

huge cone just begging me to eat it. I opened my mouth
wide took a big bite and . . . there was nothing there. No ice
cream, no flavor, nothing.

That, too, woke me up. That dream did not repeat.

Joseph, diviner of dreams, where are you when we need
you?

Let's step out of the police station and dreams and into
the halls of business and those who labor therein with and
without unions . . .

The Good Lord

We were ready to pack it in. Nearly 2:00 A.M. and the night shift at the *Hammond Times* was ready to head for the barn. Back then—in June, 1964—it was an afternoon newspaper, so the bulk of the staff reported early in the morning and tried to beat an absolute deadline of 9:30.

Herb Lukens, great reporter, an original member of the Corinthian Press Club in Cincinnati, Ohio, Gus Rose and me were the entire shift lorded over by night City Editor Jim Brahos.

We were headed for the exit when Herb said, "What's making light flicker on the walls?

I looked up, trotted to a back window and saw a raging fire.

The *Times* building fronted Fayette Street in Hammond and the next block north was Sibley Boulevard. One block east of our location, on Sibley, was the four building interconnected complex of The First Baptist Church.

I said, "The First Baptist Church is on fire."

That was no small pronouncement. The First Baptist Church of Hammond had 4,100 members. There were 2,000 members in its Sunday School. Both were the biggest in the state of Indiana.

Gus and me hit the pavement running.

The fire turned out to be an ordinary six-hour-run-of-the-mill fight by spray drenched firemen using seven trucks and three aerial units trying to save what they could.

The thing that made it interesting was that two old buildings, one east and the other west of a new 2,000 seat auditorium, burned to the ground and the new building was practically undamaged!

Fire Chief Edward Spolnik said he thought the buildings might have been torched.

The Very Reverend Jack Hyles, leader of the solemn multitude, said services would be held in the new auditorium—dedicated just eight weeks earlier—the next Sunday and the Sunday School Building and the Old Church destroyed by the fire would be rebuilt.

I was putting my story on the hook when our day City Editor Clint Wilkinson strolled up and queried, "What did God's rep here on earth say about the unusual configuration of the gutted buildings?"

Gus had interviewed the Rev. Hyles, so I yelled over to him with the question. Gus said, "Didn't ask."

Clint, a hair on the lee side of boiling over, said too quietly to me, "Find out."

At that time I had a private listing of unlisted numbers. This was a hangover from my ten years as a radio reporter when there was no other reporter to turn to when you had an on air broadcast and you had to reach someone in a hurry. I never entered an office or home with an unlisted number that I didn't jot down or memorize the number showing on the dial. No touchtone equipment back then.

So, I had the Rev's private, unlisted phone number dating to a time when he wanted some propaganda written about a church project (a youth summer camp, as I remember). I was invited into his office.

See above.

I dialed the number. He answered the call undoubtedly thinking it was anything but a reporter. I asked the question immediately putting the little great man on both prongs of a dilemma. He knew if he didn't answer, I would so write. But he also knew he couldn't tell the truth. So he took it to a higher level: He said, *"The Lord moves in mysterious ways his miracles to perform!"* and hung up.

I added the quote to my copy on the hook and went home.

When I checked in at 6:00 that evening, I skimmed the story and noticed my quote was not a part of the report.

I asked Night City Editor Jim Brahos if he knew what happened to my Hyles quote.

"Clint said it was too trite to print," he said. "You're roving tonight. Cophouse, St. Margaret's emergency room, and, hey, don't forget that motorcycle bunch down there in back of the Interlude Lounge. Find out if that 6-foot three inch tall girl is really gonna help Harley design cycles for women. How many 6'3" women are there waiting to buy Harleys?"

As for not using the exclusive quote, it was alright with me. I didn't even know if Hyles got it right.

This was part of my thoughts as a reporter. Once I put a piece on the hook I didn't care what the editors did with it. As far as I was concerned I had done my job. I seldom even read what appeared in the paper unless some irate reader called and complained I had gotten something wrong or left out the name of a key player or some such. In that case I would ask the critic to hang on while I got a copy and we'd work it out. An explanation of what I had written and why almost always did the trick.

My only request was that if editors changed the story materially they would not hang my by-line on it. All the editors respected that request except one. That one later became the Managing Editor of the *Times of Northwest Indiana.*

Go figure!

While we're on the subject of fires . . .

Not Meant for Daylight

We all heard the BOOM through the partially sealed doors of the *Times* editorial room on Hammond, Indiana's Fayette Street and had time to look at each other before the police radio began yelling for fire fighting assistance at the fireworks plant in Melrose Park, Illinois. That would make it about twelve miles west of the paper.

City Editor Clint Wilkinson said, "Gary Three" and I moved. The two other Garys on the staff had been there longer than me, so I was Gary Three by default.

There was a pen in my shirt pocket and paper in the car for note taking purposes and I kept boots, a warm old coat and a hard hat in the trunk so there was no reason to delay.

It was Monday, March 6, 1972, and there was still a winter chill in the air. I was glad I hadn't had time to put the cold weather gear away.

The second blast—a much bigger one—shook the ground as I crossed to Illinois on 165th Street headed west with some concern about how this assignment might affect my longevity. That second explosion was discouraging.

Later it was determined it shattered windows in a five mile radius of the plant.

There were three more concussions of varying intensity before squad cars blocked me near the intersection of Routes 405 and 6 in Orland Park. That's about a mile east of the Melrose Park Display Fireworks Company plant.

The "war zone" look of the surroundings began about three miles further back. The company was really putting on a colorful daylight display for its neighbors.

I parked the car where the very important, in charge, uniformed Palos Park policeman, was pointing and headed for the corner wondering immediately why everybody was stopped so far from the scene.

I found out from Winnie Frank of Winnie's Restaurant fame located on the northeast corner of the intersection.

"Dynamite," she said. "They've got tons of it in underground bunkers between here and the plant. That goes, we might be too close."

Her words carried some weight since she was standing on glass shards and talking to me through a display window that had once had that glass in it.

Across the street at the Virginia Motor Court Motel I noted triple parked fire trucks from Chicago Ridge, Oak Lawn, North Palos, Roberts Park, Hometown, Nottingham Park, Bridgeview and Bedford Park. Further west, with binoculars borrowed from a bystander, I could make out through the haze fire engines pumping water at something that once may have been a building. They belonged to Orland Park, Posen, Palos Park and Tinley Park.

The whole area smelled like someone had just touched off a firecracker next to me.

Well, the police wouldn't let me get any closer, and officials weren't holding any news conferences, so I became interested in a fire hose leading the other way—back east away from the action. It just seemed natural to follow it and find out the reason for this seemingly wasted effort. And about a half mile east at Routes 6 and 104 a fire truck so new the number hadn't been painted on it yet, was pulling water out of a small nameless creek and sending it down 104 to be relayed on to the trucks at the fight scene. Of course! Who would put a fire hydrant near a fireworks company?

Melven Snyder was tending the rig. He looked worried and very busy so I didn't bother him for more than his name.

I strolled back to the corner where Winnie and her employee Linda Richey were handing out coffee on the house to firemen, cops and anyone else who needed it.

Bob LaMantia, who knew he was too close for safety if the dynamite let go, was watching pressure gauges on a pumper and looked cold and uneasy. Turns out he could see his house from where he stood and was concerned about structural damage.

"I got bounced out of bed when it exploded," he told me. "Went and got the engine and came here. I didn't have time to check the house, but all the pictures were off the walls and the windows broke." He was relieved about three hours later and went home to check it out.

How bad was it? Ask four-year-old Dawn Andresen. She was asleep on the couch in her home when the second blast leveled the factory.

Her mother, Nancy, could tell her the fireworks plant blew up because she had been alerted by the earlier explosion. "I don't see how she slept through that first shot," she told me, "but that second hammer would have woke up the folks over in the cemetery."

Their home was four miles from "ground zero."

More than 30 people told me that long afternoon about the tons of dynamite they knew were buried near where they stood. I quoted the people already mentioned in this story along with restaurant employee Alice Lund, Ted Curtis of Lake Shore Oil Co., who was supervising the boarding up of broken windows, and filling station owners Frank Stone and Larry Moody. They all feared "the great one" for more than four hours that afternoon.

The next day fireworks company owner Anthony Cartolano denied the existence of any stored dynamite. He had lost his father and an uncle during a similar disaster at the company in 1955 and was known to be meticulously careful about safety. Still, his firm made the huge canisters of powder for displays at the White Sox games, Holiday displays and other celebrations nationwide. He had to store materials somewhere, so I still believe the people. I also think the event proved the safety of the bunkers, but in order to calm the residents in towns surrounding the plant—the *Times* ran a skinback.

The only time in more than 30 years of news reporting anything I wrote was retracted!

Two died. The owner probably didn't need any more grief.

Details in the paper Tuesday, March 7, 1972. It's the skylight story on the front page along with a very good multiple photo spread by camera craftsman Al Vanderver showing the devastation of the area.

Sometimes a very small spark affects a whole lot of people.

Doomsday in Andover

Andover, Ohio, was known in the mid-1950s as the "Gateway to the Pymatuning," a resort and vacation area in northeastern Ohio south and east of Ashtabula.

I was working at WICA AM, FM and TV in the latter town and preparing for the switch over from the radio side to the evening TV duties when the station shook with the explosion some twenty miles away.

The Rowley Brothers owned not only the broadcast facilities, but also the *Ashtabula Star Beacon, Painsville Telegraph, Conneat News Herald* and *Geneva Free Press* newspapers. Most of the newspaper headlines back at the time were lifted almost word for word from my local newscasts. So I knew they would want this one.

I grabbed the Webcor reel-to-reel tape recorder (thirty-five pounds), yelled at Charley Mandrake to take the news and weather, ran to the parking lot and headed south. I soon found myself part of a parade of squad cars, fire trucks and other emergency vehicles headed south in a hurry. To me it was scary. Have you ever driven eighty miles per hour twenty feet in back of the car in front of you with hopes nothing happens to it or any of the other vehicles in the high speed chain? Gave me a whole new respect for race-car chauffeurs. I arrived about the same time as Corporal Kangas of the Ohio State Highway Patrol and followed his squadroll into town.

A restaurant and ice cream parlor (the Isly Store) in the middle of the village was completely shattered. Kangas took one look and told his backups to seal the town. Nobody in or out except emergency vehicles and maybe the governor.

He looked long and hard at me, but decided to let me stay.

There were forty-four people in the place when it blew up—twenty-two survived, twenty-two didn't. The twenty-two who lived were literally thrown out of the building by the blast. Those who were not died among the shattered remains of the structure. They, along with most of the building, were now in the debris-filled former basement. That's where we all went to work including the police, able-bodied townspeople, firemen, ambulance drivers, and other available volunteers, throwing bricks out of the basement and carrying out those who never knew why fate had chosen them.

Within the first twenty-four hours we had recovered twenty of the victims. We were still throwing bricks, shattered wood, furniture and broken dishes out of the building forty-eight hours later looking for twin sixteen-year-old sisters who had been given permission by their father to go to work in the Isly store just two weeks earlier.

During a brief respite, KYW-TV in Cleveland offered me $105 per foot for sound on film coverage of the activity. To give you an idea of what that was worth, at the time I was working for $68.50 a *week*. I didn't have a movie camera, so I had to turn them down. Think what such film would be worth today.

Almost seventy-two hours after the rescue effort began, in what came to be called the Andover Disaster, volunteers were still looking for the last two people unaccounted for: the twin girls. They were found when the crew working at the time heaved enough of the debris out of the basement to clear the doors of a huge walk-in freezer located in the back wall.

When they opened the doors, the girls became the

twenty-first and twenty-second fatalities. The air sort of went out of the balloon, then. Everybody just sank to the ground where they were. No one said much. Bob Cox, who had waddled his single-engine plane to a landing in a nearby field and hiked into town the second day, whispered "Jesus Christ." We were suddenly all tired and, one by one, the men got up and walked out of history. I hurried back to my car with the intent of getting the tape recorder and interviewing some of the people, sat down to adjust the reels, and was awakened by Kangas several hours later.

He said he had stopped by to thank me for pitching in.

I did interview the furniture-store owner, who told me in one second he was in the doorway of his business watching his wife leaving the restaurant directly across the street from him and the next instant she was lying in the gutter at his feet and there was nothing behind her. He was the first to tell me he could not remember hearing an explosion.

A lady who lived with her two young sons on the second floor of the building next to the restaurant had told her two boys to finish watching their TV show and then they could go get an ice cream cone. They had been pestering her about it for several minutes. She said she was peeling potatoes at the sink and felt "a vibration." She looked up, glanced at the boys and saw their feet dangling in open air. She, of course, scooted over to them and calmly told them to crawl along the couch to her. None of the three had even a scratch.

There was, however, a huge hole in the south wall of her apartment and a good piece of floor missing.

She said she never heard a sound.

But twenty miles away everyone in the broadcast complex heard the explosion and felt the ground tremble. I sometimes wonder if the human body processes sound differently when it's too loud.

Dr. Sam Shepard of Bay Village told police his wife Marilyn's scream from her second-floor bedroom woke him up from a sound sleep on a couch in the downstairs living room of their home, but his son, asleep in the bedroom next to her with doors of both rooms open, heard nothing, nor did the family dog in the room with the boy.

This seeming contradiction went a long way in convicting Sam for murder in his first trial. That and the fact he described a mighty fight with "a bushy-haired stranger" that he accused of bludgeoning his wife to death. But, I wonder. Even if we agree there could be such a thing as a silent scream between two closely attuned people, wouldn't the fight in the hallway have awakened the boy or the dog?

Sam, his wife Marilyn, and the dog are no longer of this world. The boy, now a man the last I knew, was still searching for "the bushy-haired stranger."

As I heard, the Andover explosion was attributed to leaking natural gas. My problem with that is no one smelled the butyl mercaptin added to the odorless gas so it can be detected. Conspiracy theorists could have a ball with that one.

When I arrived back at the station, Don Fassett, the overburdened station manager, complained about the brevity of my reports from the scene. They were good enough, however, to make the front pages of the *Ashtabula Star Beacon, Painsville Telegraph, Conneat News Herald* and the *Geneva Free Press.*

This was one of the first big stories I covered, so why not follow me to one of the last before I was thrust into riding 76,000 miles on a bicycle.

How to Steal an Election

Well, I don't know how.

But if you're thinking about it you might look at Local 551 of the United Auto Workers Union on Chicago's near southside. Its members work at the Ford Motor Company assembly plant at Hegewisch, Illinois, and the parts depot in Melrose Park. Yessir, it helps if you have two or more voting locations and must move a ballot box forty-two or so miles on a dark night in January.

Gerald Vale Sr. ran for President of the 4,000-member local with his slate of thirteen candidates for various other offices against five-time incumbent President John Nolan and his group. Nolan won by a shade more than 100 votes. Vale charged the votes from the parts depot were stolen by pre-marking ballots in Nolan's favor, removing the official seal from the ballot box, freezing out his observer, and switching the ballot box on the trip to the union headquarters at 10550 Torrence Avenue, where the fraudulent votes were ultimately counted.

Nolan won the "official" tally, 1,206 to 999, with 101 votes from the parts department cast for Nolan and four for Vale. If the 105 votes were deducted from Nolan's total and added to Vale's it would swing the election to Vale, 1,104 to 1,101.

As proof of his charge the ballot box was switched, Vale pointed out all the votes from the parts plant were marked in a regular pencil, apparently by the same person, while forty-six of the men said they had made their selections with fountain pens, fourteen more said they voted for Vale, and one man claimed to have marked his ballot with a green pencil.

Please keep in mind the slates were not only gunning to head up their local, but would also be automatic delegates to the National convention of the full 750,000 member International Union meeting in Atlantic City the following fall.

So, how was it done?

First, let's get the cast of characters straight: Gene A. Middleton, Vale's rep at the parts depot; Quinton W. Knight and Daniel Wachowski, Nolan's reps; there's also one other pivotal figure here whose actual role I was never able to pin down—Richard Houba, election chairman—who was either an honest man with a flawed memory or one so inept it almost defies logic. He was the man who kept the Melrose Park votes from being mixed in with the overall union vote in the big box at union HQ, but he was also the man who set up the scenario for possible fraud by failing to protect the integrity of the Melrose Park ballot box!

According to Vale and his group the ball began when poll-watcher Middleton, appointed by Vale, wasn't allowed to ride to Melrose Park in the same car with the two watchers representing Nolan, Knight and Wachowski. This is important because it meant that Vale's watcher could be separated from the ballot box on the way back from the parts depot to union headquarters, because he would have to drive his own car.

Then at Melrose Park after the voting, Vale's rep Middleton sealed the ballot box with an official seal supplied to him for that purpose.

Witnesses said it was at this point that Wachowski made a phone call and came back to tell those present he had talked to Nolan and Nolan had told him to *remove the seal!* For some reason lost in infinity this was done!

Now you have an unsealed ballot box in the hands of

Knight and Wachowski in a car headed for the union hall followed by Vale's rep in a second car. You need a plan here to separate the two vehicles right?

Knight and Wachowski took the toll road. They had correct change. Went right through. Middleton, following, surprised, had to wait for change. Cars now apart. Did Nolan's men pull over to the large parking area at the toll booths and wait for Middleton? Be serious. They fled on ahead and stopped at an oasis for a cup of coffee and rest. Couriers carrying ballot boxes often do this sort of thing on a long forty-two-mile trip, I guess.

In the filed affidavit, Knight said Wachowski was alone with the ballot box for a few minutes while he went to the washroom. If a switch was made Wachowski did it. Everyone agreed he was the only one alone with the ballot box after it was taken from Melrose Park.

John M. Nolan was not available for comment. Not at his home, union hall, favorite club, motion picture show, miniature golf course, nowhere. The man had gone missing.

My story hit the streets February 17, 1972.

Ford Motor Company prohibited sales of the paper in its plant.

The next day, Nolan was everywhere! He was quoted as denying any shenanigans in the union vote.

Interestingly enough, Mr. Nolan in a two-hour interview the following day never addressed any of the charges. Sound familiar?

Here is an indication of what Mr. Nolan sold the public the next day: he said the people should be criticizing those who were making the outcry. He indicated the National Union's Solidarity House would investigate the charges and his local would back the investigation in every way possible.

Solidarity House, in Detroit, in the person of William J. Beckman, Administrative Assistant to the President of the

UAW, acknowledged the formal complaint by Vale, Casey Kocinski, Financial Secretary candidate and Henry Reed, candidate for Recording Secretary.

From that point the thing became an internal example of digestion by any huge entity which has little incentive to care about any breach that costs them less than their seat in a $5,000 leather chair and a high six-figure income. The holes in this story are as big as those left by the death of JFK or the firestorm at Waco. What was Houba's role? Yes, his ruling kept the Parts Depot vote separate from the rest of the ballots when traditionally all the votes were mixed together, but he also "forgot" to relay a request to let Vale's man Middleton ride in the same car with Nolan's Knight and Wachowski. And was Middleton really naïve enough to remove an official seal from the ballot box on Wachowski's report of a phone call?

And was Nolan Ford Motor Company's pet union leader? I neither saw nor heard of them preventing sale of the paper carrying Nolan's disclaimer of fraud in their plant. Their reason for suspending sale of the paper carrying the story charging switched ballots in the union election was, they said, that they didn't want the company to look like a part of union activity.

Seemed to this reporter they were at least either trying to protect Nolan and his incumbent slate over Vale's group, or maybe feared a clash between the two parties' backers if the news hit on the factory floor. Maybe not, but. . . .

My experience has been that it is at least as hard to remove an elected union officer from office as it is to defeat an Industrial Chief Executive Officer of a corporation or an incumbent public official, no matter how inept they prove to be. I refer you to the masters of such publicly traded firms as Enron, General Motors, and Lucent, to name a few, along with such shining stars as "Teddy" Kennedy, "Fast Eddy"

Radoliak, and (my personal favorite) Bill Clinton. None did anything that reduced their own power, prestige or personal fortunes.

Of course there's always the successful ones, like Bill Gates, Lee Iacocca and the man who almost singlehandedly made the Teamsters Union the wealthiest and most powerful in the nation . . . Jimmy Hoffa.

Look what happened to them. Two out of three were cast out, one permanently, one sidetracked to retirement, and one smart enough to bow to the majority's game.

Forty dogs bring down the wolf. Play the duplication game or be bled to death. Fifty-seven thousand police agencies, more than 240 suburbs in Chicago alone, within counties within states within America. Trouble is, this duplication means no one is really responsible for anything.

As a reporter my life was threatened by followers of Gary, Indiana's first African-American mayor because I had questioned the fact he had received more than two *billion* tax payer dollars and no one could tell me where the money was or what it had been spent on. The letters promised my death, the death of my family members, and bodily harm to anyone I had even shook hands with in the past twenty years.

I met with two agents of the F.B.I. at a local restaurant. They told me to see the Hammond Police because the radio station was in Hammond. The Hammond Police referred me to the police in the town I lived in who, in turn, told me since I worked in one town and lived in another I should talk with the county sheriff's office wherein was located both villages.

I decided to continue their silly game.

Sheriff's deputies—two of them in my living room—told me since the threats were mailed I should take my problem to the Postal Inspector. Somebody at the post office in Chicago told me this was a case for the, uh huh, F.B.I.

Bam! Full circle. I called one of the agents I had first met with, and told him of the runaround with various agencies and he advised me to arm myself, keep an irregular schedule, and call back if I found a suspect for them to question. Maybe I should have called the female agent.

Well, a microphone opened at 6:00 A.M. for me every day except Sunday and I was expected to say something. So much for an irregular schedule. And I was not going to have a suspect unless something happened to my family or my own comfort.

I had no trouble getting a permit to carry. The weapon cost the Kansas farm boy more than $400 in 1980 and helped me lose my job. The weapon scared the pulp out of a co-worker when I took my coat off in the newsroom.

So much for Bill Clinton's 100,000 additional policemen (women), a Drug Enforcement Agency, Alcohol, Tobacco and Firearms, Federal Bureau of Investigation, Border Patrol, Postal Inspectors, Secret Service, Sheriff's Departments, Town Marshals, yatta ta yatta ta.

See, no one's responsible.

Officials know how to make *you* responsible, though! Forget to file your income tax and it's your fault. Mail it and let the post office lose it and it's your fault. Let someone get hit by a meteorite carrying it to his bench and it's your fault. So they know how. They also know how to avoid responsibility. Quick, anybody know the identity of the sniper who fired a bullet through the head of a woman *holding a baby in a doorway at Ruby Ridge?* Or who was calling the shots when federal agents could have just arrested the cult leader near Waco, Texas, when he went into town for a loaf of bread?

These, dear folks, are not isolated incidents.

We are seriously nearing the time when it is imperative

we hold faceless appointed bureaucrats responsible for their actions. Can it be done? Is there still time? Fifty percent, half, the union workers in America are employees of the various governments. That's fairly difficult to overcome. Good luck!

Today the national news is mostly either a direct reading or a rewrite of the Associated Press "A" wire. There is no United Press or International News Service and Reuter's must be rewritten. That's why you hear the same words and terms in a news story no matter who is presenting it to you. News in America, other than the very local, is a monopoly.

You can challenge it—the official version—but if you win you lose.

I know. I beat their deceptions three times and lost the city administration, police department, and the courts as sources for news. I, personally, would do it again. I'm proud of the fact I made culprits pay. But mostly I'm proud of the fact that in almost thirty years of reporting news I cannot remember once asking anyone: *How does it feel?*

May you be clothed in peace and beauty!

Just For Fun

In some of the previous stories contained herein there were instances of what some might term luck, or coincidence or possibly the intervention of a higher power or force to save my more expensive parts. This type of occurrence was not unusual for me and I thought a few examples might clarify the point and amuse some of you who also marvel at these seeming little miracles. When they happened to me I always asked:

What are the odds?

As a young broadcaster in 1955 I was selected to host a remote show from the large Pontiac dealership in Ashtabula, Ohio. My car was a 1949 Ford two-door I had rebuilt while working nights at the Schreiber Trucking relay station in Bowling Green. At WICA AM, FM and TV I was making $85 a week.

Looking at the sleek new Pontiac Star Chief convertible sparkling among the new cars on display, I remember thinking there was no way I'd ever be driving a car like it.

Three months later the little '49 Ford had moved me, my wife, baby daughter and a U-Haul trailer to Gary, Indiana, for a new job and I had rented an apartment in the Miller area of the Steel City from a man named Jim Geer.

Three weeks after we moved in, Geer approached me and offered a deal. He'd been laid off from his city job, he said, and he couldn't meet both the house and car payments. "Pick up the car payments, throw in your car so I'll have something to get around in and we'll do the deal."

The next day I was driving a new Pontiac Star Chief convertible *exactly* like the one I thought I'd never own.

What are the odds?

Richard Pontney, Advertising Director for Montgomery Ward and Company in Gary's Village Shopping Center, asked me to meet Anacha von Braun, the Tulip Queen from Holland, and interview her. Seems she was touring the U.S. for the retailer promoting the sale of flowers.

I agreed immediately, met her, did the interview and was ready to depart the airport when Dick invited me to join the group for lunch at the Hotel Gary. I happily accepted and during the meal Anacha told me she was interested in sports and jazz and asked if I had played in any games. I told her some in high school and mentioned one of the odd experiences was watching my team get clobbered gracefully in football by the team from Middletown, Ohio.

"I can still close my eyes and picture the linemen coming around end, in sync, perfectly balanced in rhythm," I told her.

"You know why?" the lady accompanying Miss von Braun spoke up.

I said, "Actually, no, I don't."

"Well," she purred, "I'm from Middletown, Ohio, and I had two boys who played football. They were *required* to take two years of ballet training. No dance lessons, no football! Of course, it was a deep dark secret because none of the boys wanted it known they took dance lessons."

I was stunned! Not from what she told me, but that she was there to tell me and that I had mentioned the trivial incident to Anacha. I couldn't remember telling anyone about the grace of the Middletown team since I had left Dayton eleven years before. I also didn't know why I told it to

Anacha. That was weird enough, but to have someone there who knew the reason was unbelievable!

I had to wait eleven years and meet the Tulip Queen from Holland in Gary, Indiana, to find out why my high school team was gracefully beaten by the boys from Middletown.

What are the odds?

I lost my left eye in a boxing accident in 1946 so for most of my life no big industry would consider hiring me. The exception was the Northern Indiana Public Service Company. John Clark, Assistant to Vice President James F. Purcell of Public Relations, was retiring and he had suggested me as his replacement.

Mr. Clark called me at the *Times,* Mr. Purcell interviewed me and offered me the job. The company doctor gave me 100 percent on the mandated physical exam with the notation I was blind in the left eye.

Enter, center stage, Walter Hathaway, Manager of Industrial Relations (employment) who without talking to me found himself highly insulted. Others told me he said I should have failed the physical because of the eye, then hired with the proviso that I had special needed skills.

I was a pup in corporate politics and didn't realize at the time how serious this was. Hathaway felt he had been bypassed. A sacred fiefdom had been tromped on and he couldn't let it stand. Had I been more experienced in corporate layers of authority, I would have seen the danger more quickly and reacted.

As it was he did everything he could behind my back to make it hard for me to do my job and I was just blithely unaware of it all.

At every turn for four years, Walt Hathaway never let up. He had Margaret Byerly, who assigned all the secretaries, send me beautiful but incompetent, untrained, and un-interested girls. My asking for an experienced middle-aged woman who could handle appointments, record keeping, contact lists, make arrangements for trips I had to take to New York, Romulus, Michigan, New Orleans, San Jose, Burbank, etc., went unfulfilled. I created the company employee newspaper and he told other managers not to report news of their districts and divisions to me. He tried to get engineers to give me false information to represent to the outside press. I could go on with examples of his underhanded treachery for several pages, but point made.

In the fifth year of my tenure at NIPSCO word filtered up that Walt Hathaway, with no such problem for forty years, had *lost an eye!*

I never found out how and I don't know why.

What are the odds?

The first girl I can remember regarding seriously was Marilyn Miller. We were both in the 8th grade at E.J. Brown School and I figured she was perfection.

Unfortunately she had no reciprocal thoughts for me.

And to add flames to my kindling, she began dating a little bowlegged runt from Texas—accent and all.

So, one night, to see what they would do, I hid in the bushes outside Marilyn's house and watched the hug at the end of their date. The next day sharp-eyed Marilyn had her mother call my mother to tell me not to spy on her. I never again went near or spoke to her.

Then one afternoon, four years later, strolling home from high school a week before graduation, Marilyn was suddenly walking beside me with a bright "Hello," and most winning smile. She asked my after graduation plans tripping lightly ahead of me and walking backwards. I told her four more years of school toiling at Bowling Green State University.

We came to Catalpa Drive and a parting of the ways.

Two years later I was home in Dayton to say goodbye to my folks who were moving to California where Dad had taken a job with an aircraft company to work on the Pogo Stick (vertical takeoff) and Sea Dart (a prototype navy jet). I was just there for the weekend, one of the few times home from college except for vacations. I would have to return to Bowling Green for Monday classes.

So it turned out on a Saturday afternoon my mother asked me to run up to the new supermarket a block-and-a-half north on Main Street for a quart of milk. Neither Dad nor Mom were milk drinkers and she hadn't expected me to turn up so there was none in the house.

I went to the store, got my quart of milk and turned the corner of an aisle and was looking directly at the swollen belly of an eight months pregnant Marilyn. I smiled and said, "Hi Marilyn." She collapsed to the floor and began laughing uncontrollably. When the little man came running up (apparently not a Texan), I assumed her husband, the laughter turned to tears. I just said "Hi" to her. I told him so long, and got out of Dodge.

The two to three minutes I was in that store that day was the only time I ever saw the place. Didn't know it existed before that day, never returned to it after that day.

What are the odds?

Charley Muro literally rode shotgun for the biggest gambling house in northern Ohio a quarter mile south of the Michigan State line. His station was on a walkway ten feet or so above the floor. He was a very well paid, happy man sitting above the crowd holding his shotgun, but worried how his daughter who was about to enter high school would feel if the place was raided and her father was cited for unlawful activity. So he took his worry to his boss.

The boss solved the problem by making him manager of the Shalimar Room of the Commodore Perry Hotel in downtown Toledo.

As such matters are wont to happen, I had taken a young lady to the Shalimar Room and left a gold-colored cigarette lighter on the table when we left. Naturally I went back the next day to see if I could retrieve it. Charley had it waiting for me, refused a tip and we shook hands. I escorted dates to his room from time to time and we became nodding acquaintances until one day in the record library at the university forever changed our relationship.

"What are you doing with that?" the very striking young dark-haired lady said in a no-nonsense tone.

"With what?" I asked, searching for wiggle room.

"That record," she said. I was holding Paul Whiteman's recording of "Cho Cho San," his orchestra's jazzed up version of the heroine's song from *Madama Butterfly.*

"I'm listing it for my show tonight." I pointed to the song sheet.

"Oh no!" the young lady protested. "I need that record for *my* show!!"

I mumbled something about the laws of possession and she tore me apart with a forlorn look and the words, "It'll ruin my show if I don't have that record."

She got the record. I bought her a fried baloney sandwich at Puts and Pats and she granted me a date for the following Saturday night.

Which is why I was tooling up the Dixie Highway between Toledo and Detroit looking for an address when I spotted Charley in a front yard trimming a bush. I pulled over and said "Hey, Charley, you live here?"

He said yes and asked why I was in his neighborhood. "I

got a date with this girl Joyce Muro who lives up this way," I told him. "I was looking for her address when I spotted you."

"Yeah, my daughter. Come on in."

No, I had never taken Joyce to the Shalimar room—she was more of an Ohio State Fair, horse racing, visit friends type of girl. As a result I unknowingly knew the father of my wife of 19,689 days for two years before I met her!

What are the odds?

Zimmerman (I don't know his first name) was, I was advised, for many years one of the brilliant photographers for *Time-Life*. I, then with WJOB news, got on my horse for the Gary Airport when word was flashed that Vice Presidential candidate Henry Cabot Lodge was injured in South Bend while boarding a plane for Gary.

Nobody knew how badly and back then planes in flight lacked "ship to shore" communications.

When his plane landed in Gary, I trapped the candidate and his wife on the stairs as they came out of the airship and interviewed him about the injury.

It turned out to be negligible.

All the time the ten-minute interview was going on I could hear a photographer in the background saying things like, "Who's the SOB in the shirt? Get the guy in the shirt out of there!" and so on interlaced with language more suited to a longshoreman. My report, in July, 1960, was the first word of the candidate's injury.

Ten years later while acting as Manager of Press Relations for the Northern Indiana Public Service Company I received a call from the manager of the Bailly Generating Station.

"I got a guy with a camera here wants to climb one of our towers to take a shot of Bethlehem Steel," he said. "Can we let him?"

"Who is he?" I requested.

After a short pause the manager came back on the phone and said, "Says he's Zimmerman. . . ."

I said, "Put him on."

When the photog greeted me I told him I was Gary Wilson. Without pause Zimmerman said, "I don't get to climb the tower do I?"

Yes he did after the automatic warnings and signing an injury waiver, but what amazed me was the situation itself.

From WJOB to the *Hammond Times* to NIPSCO to be in position to call the shots on a guy who had growled at me years before was unbelievable.

What are the odds?

George "Mel" Whitney was one hell of an engineer. When I went to work for him at WGRY in Gary he equipped my car with a Motorola Transmitter in the trunk, a pre-amp in the glove compartment and a low impedance microphone. He also included a hundred feet of mike cable.

I could broadcast from anywhere in a fifty-mile radius of the station with studio quality sound from my car. And I could get close to interview personalities anywhere that most other reporters couldn't reach.

So when word was released that Queen Elizabeth would visit Buckingham Fountain in Chicago during a tour of the Great Lakes to mark the opening of the St. Lawrence Seaway, I headed for the fountain to scope out the territory.

When I reached it I parked nearby, looked up and *here comes the Queen!* She was striding toward the fountain flanked by four red vested, tall, lean bodyguards with the eighteen-inch beaver hats and with Prince Phillip strolling along about six steps in back of her.

I flipped on the power, grabbed the mike and started trotting for the Queen. With every step I took the body guards closed ranks toward her by six inches until with an almost casual small wave of her hand they dropped back.

My first words were "Welcome to America, Your Highness. I hear you carry your own water."

I had read somewhere that there was a 400-gallon tank of drinking water on the royal yacht for the Queen so her complexion would not be altered by a change. She chuckled, affirmed the tank was on board and granted me a fifteen-minute interview.

She is one charming lady. I don't know if she thought she was talking to a reporter from one of Chicago's 50,000 watt torches or not, but she treated me like I was.

When I got back to the little daytime-only "teakettle" station I found most of that interview was lost because our remote frequency was shared with Inland Steel and they had priority since their communications might involve employee safety.

It was sometime later that I realized I had met the Queen on a trial run of her own when a fellow reporter asked me how I got through the crowd.

There was no crowd when I was there an hour ahead of the formal press conference!

What are the odds?

Oil, A Play on Words

There was once a science fiction story about a space ship traveling to a distant galaxy titled *A Little Oil.* It told the story that everyone aboard the craft had a job, pilot, engineer, cook, child bearer, obvious to everybody—with one exception. There was this no-talent guy that no one could figure out. However, as the story unfolded it became obvious that when people became angry, were ready to clobber each other, this cat would step in, tell a joke and smooth things over for everybody.

A little oil.

In Hammond, Indiana, during the 1960s, Sam Miller was that guy. He managed the Civic Center where the circus came to town, the western bands played, and the basketball tournament was held. He ran a bail bond service on the side and smoothed things between the officials and various citizens who ran nefarious businesses.

So, it was no surprise when Connie Samios, a great photographer, and I were lunching with Sam in John's Restaurant that Sam's pager spoke up. He excused himself, made a phone call, and returned to tell us he would have to leave. "Enjoy your meal," he said, "I gotta go take care of something."

"Anything newsworthy?" I inquired.

"No, just the same old thing. Somebody forgot to make a payoff or paid the wrong amount or was out of town. I'll take care of it," he said. "One hand does not wash itself."

So, now you know Sam and why I said "ok" when he invited me to accompany him to a joint on State Line Avenue:

"You can watch the strippers, kid, while I see if a client of mine trying to skip bail is visiting his girl friend."

We walked in and there was a surprise for both of us that had nothing to do with Sam's business.

Me first: a friend of mine was making a complete fool of himself over one of the strippers. It was strictly lewd and raunchy even for sin city.

Now Sam. "Hey kid, see those two guys over there. Their day job is with Standard Oil of Indiana, but their night job is undercover agents with the Calumet City Police. This perfumed boudoir is going to be hit! Let's move outta here."

"Gimme a minute," I requested. "I need to throw a friend a life jacket."

I was able to tear my buddy away from his loud enticement of the stripper long enough to warn him of impending disaster. He ignored my advice and returned to his suggestions as to what the girl could do with various body parts with his help.

Sam and me, however, exited the place *"tout sweet"* as they say in villages across the Atlantic and walked half a block north to Angelo's Restaurant at the corner of State Line and State Street, which eatery had a booth on the southeast corner jutting out so a person could look back down State Line.

We were there maybe five minutes when the sirens and bubble lights went off and the place was shut down by about a dozen Cal City cops.

My friend was arrested, charged with soliciting, publicly identified, divorced, and out of town within six weeks.

Fourteen years later, after finishing the Elroy-Sparta bicycle trail in Wisconsin, me and a friend were peddling into a park to set up our tent for the night when a voice yelled GARY WILSON!

It was the man from the strip club sitting in front of the

largest damn mobile home I had ever seen. Turns out he visited that remote park once every two years making his rounds as a cheese salesman. We had a beer, brought each other up to date, and I left to rejoin my riding partner. I never saw or spoke to him again. I was never in that remote park before in my life or since that night. We waved goodbye in the morning.

What are the odds?

I can't leave this without a tip for cyclists. They don't call it Elroy-Sparta for nothing. Peddle from Sparta to Elroy and the last twelve miles is a three percent grade uphill!

Looking back I sometimes feel it would have been wise to request Sam for a little of his "oil" in convincing my friend to exit the tinsel castle of erotic ladies. But, if I had done so, this book would no doubt have featured a very different ending.

Make yourself comfortable.